ADVENTURES IN YELLOWSTONE

"Entertaining, thought-provoking and educational ... A revelation for kids and parents alike."
DICK DURBIN
U.S. Senator (D-IL)

"A great achievement ..."
ROBERT F. KENNEDY, JR.

"Reminded me of all the books I loved so much as a kid."
MARTHA MARKS
Co-Founder and President, Republicans for Environmental Protection

"The investment you make in buying this book will return interest to the planet for generations to come."
FRANCES BEINECKE
President, Natural Resources Defense Council

"This series will fascinate young readers ..."
LARRY SCHWEIGER
President and CEO, National Wildlife Federation

"A wonderful book ..."
NELL NEWMAN
Co-Founder and President, Newman's Own Organics

MOONBEAM CHILDREN'S BOOK AWARD	BENJAMIN FRANKLIN BOOK AWARD
• Best First Book (GOLD) • Pre-Teen Fiction–Intermediate/ Middle Grade (SILVER)	• Best First Book (SILVER) 

Book 1 is also a **MOM'S CHOICE AWARDS®** (SILVER) recipient for best juvenile & young adult historical fiction. The **MOM'S CHOICE AWARDS®** recognizes the best in family-friendly media and products, while the Benjamin Franklin and Moonbeam Children's Book Awards highlight the best within the independent publishing world. We are honored to be recipients of these awards.

LOST IN YELLOWSTONE

"A captivating adventure story that inspires a sense of wonder."
RICHARD LOUV
Author, Last Child in the Woods

"Use this book to foster a preservation ethic in the most important generation — the next generation."
SCOT MCELVEEN
President, Association of National Park Rangers   www.anpr.org

"Captures the thrill of good literature as a vehicle for that enticement, excitement, and curiosity of our national treasures by the next generation."
BRIAN A. DAY
Executive Director, North American Association for Environmental Education

"A brilliant job of weaving history with exciting adventure. This book inspires young people to be the change they want to see."
MIKE MEASE
Co-Founder, Buffalo Field Campaign

Buffalo Field Campaign
http://www.buffalofieldcampaign.org

"Well researched and written and true to historical events and people. *The Land of Curiosities* should be of great interest to children and young adults—and even adults. I especially enjoyed the 'Real History' facts and figures."
BRIAN SHOVERS
Library Manager, Montana Research Center

INDEPENDENT PUBLISHER BOOK AWARD	NAUTILUS BOOK AWARD
• Juvenile and Young Adult Fiction (BRONZE)	• Teen Fiction (SILVER)

Additional awards include MOONBEAM CHILDREN'S BOOK AWARD (SILVER), and MOM'S CHOICE AWARDS® (SILVER) for best young adult historical fiction.

2nd Edition Published by The EcoSeekers™
Copyright © 2015 by Little Green Dreams, LLC
d/b/a The EcoSeekers™

First edition Published 2009

Art direction and book design by Paula Winicur
Interior illustrations by David Erickson
Cover illustration by Tom Newsom
Map illustration by David Lowe

10 9 8 7 6 5 4 3 2

The text of this book is set in Parango.
Manufactured and printed in the United States of America.

This book is printed on Forest Stewardship Council
certified paper, using soy-based ink.

The EcoSeekers™ is a proud member of the Green Press Initiative.

ISBN: 978-0-9798800-8-7 / 978-0-9798800-9-4

LAND OF CURIOSITIES
BOOK 2
1872-1873

LOST
in *Yellowstone*

Written by
DEANNA NEIL

Conceived and produced by
DAVID NEIL

the ecoseekers™

Jed, Mattie, James, and Alice

~ Table of Contents ~

~ *Chapter 1* ~
CAPTURED

Alice sat on a gray, jagged rock next to a blazing camp-fire as the darkness of night ominously encircled her. Her thin dress was meager protection against the gusty mountain winds. A coarse rope, tied around her ankles, scraped against her skin whenever she moved. She hunched her shoulders and nibbled on the meat of a rabbit leg that the Long Coat Gang had thrown at her. She hated eating animals, but she knew the only other option was starvation.

"Come on, Farley," Slinger encouraged, "let's finish her off!" Farley ripped a bite of meat from a bone of the rabbit and considered Alice's fate. Farley had taken control of the Long Coat Gang after the recent death of their leader, Billy "Bloody" Knuckles. The rest of the men glared at Alice. The fire crackled and reflected against the faces of her maniacal captors, as if their skin glowed and throbbed with molten lava.

There weren't very many of them, but the few men who held Alice captive were menacing enough to frighten even a grown man. There was Steel-Fist Farley, the new leader, Charley Slinger, his sidekick, two more ruffians, and Red, the thirteen-year-old red-headed son of the deceased Bloody Knuckles.

Steel-Fist Farley and Charley Slinger were a perfect pair for trouble. Farley's nickname suited him well. He had thick, muscular hands that clenched quickly into punching devices. His jaw was square and his bulky shoulders sat like a box on his frame. His shoulders were so big that Alice swore he looked like one of the apes she had learned about at school. Farley sat by the fire at night and constantly sharpened his knife on a leather strap. Back and forth. Back and forth. He paused only to puff tobacco.

Charley Slinger was tall and gangly with a sunken chin and bulging eyes. He had tangled brown hair and reminded Alice of the yapping, little dogs she saw strolling Fifth Avenue with their wealthy owners.

But Slinger was more stretched out and scruffier than those dogs, with a stupidity that was dangerous. Alice felt impossibly far away from that life in New York now. The fire snapped, slowly sending embers floating into the sky. Wolves howled in the distance.

There were so many strange events that had led her to this place, shivering on a stone in the wilderness. Alice thought about her father dying in the Civil War, and how her family had felt shattered without his presence. She thought of her mother, Mattie, and her stepfather, Jed, the circuit-riding preacher whom her mother married several years after Alice's father had passed away. *Well, he's what got us out to Montana,* Alice reflected. From their homestead in Bozeman, Montana, the family had found their way down to Yellowstone National Park in 1872. *And that was all my fault,* she thought. Even though the trip to the park was under the guise of a holiday, it was really to let Alice "take the waters" at the hot springs in the hopes of healing her lungs. Many people believed the waters had healing properties, and the family had been willing to try anything to help ease Alice's continual discomfort and quiet her cough. As she thought of her lungs, Alice took in a deep breath and let out a long wheezy stream of air.

"We can use her to bribe her family for money. I know those Cliftons have money. I think they're related to a senator," Red said, his scarred upper lip trembling. *What a horrible boy,* Alice thought to herself.

"Time for revenge, Red! Think of what her brother did to your father. That Clifton boy killed him! Long live Bloody Knuckles!" Slinger shouted, raising up his gnawed rabbit bone with his gangly arm.

Alice looked at the cold earth and recalled how she had been captured by the gang. She had heard that Bloody Knuckles died at the hand of her own brother, James. Shocked, she then ran to find James, but she unwittingly wandered too close to the Long Coat Gang's camp at Mammoth Hot Springs. They spotted Alice as they were packing up to leave. They grabbed her and hightailed out with Alice as their prisoner. *If I hadn't wandered so close to their camp,* she thought, *they wouldn't have seen me at all.*

Red took a stick and poked sharply at the fire. The orange flames danced in his cold eyes.

"I still think we should have gone after her brother James instead," Red commented quietly.

"It's done. She's already taken, that's revenge enough. Now maybe we can make some money off

her," Farley analyzed, considering Red's advice. Alice hated how they talked about her like she wasn't present, but she felt relieved that they might not kill her.

"I can think of a few people who might buy a girl to care for their place.... How old did you say she was, Red?" Farley said, clenching his thick jaws.

"I think about eleven."

"Are you eleven?" Farley asked. The crickets sounded in the darkness. Alice didn't answer. She glanced at Red.

"Mr. Farley is speaking to you!" Slinger's eyes bulged, and he took a rabbit bone and threw it at Alice's legs.

She nodded, then started to shiver. She let out a raspy cough.

Red came over and brought an extra blanket and put it on Alice's shoulders. She wrapped it around herself abruptly, out of necessity, and then spit on the ground at his feet. Red stepped back, offended.

"She's a feisty one, alright," one of the gang said.

"Well, she better not get too feisty," Farley said. "Or else." He ran his finger across his throat. Alice shuddered at the gesture.

As hard as she tried, she couldn't stop the tears from coming. Alice had never been this scared in her life. The enchanted forests of Yellowstone had suddenly turned into fearsome woodlands, filled with malicious men and hungry animals. She longed for her mother's warm, protective arms.

"Aw, look, you made her cry," Slinger said to Farley. Alice let her food fall to the ground as she buried her face in her arms.

The gang prepared for sleep. Farley tied Alice's hands, leaving her on the frigid rock. The ropes cut into her skin as she wriggled her way down toward the fire to stay warm for the night. She had exhausted herself from crying, and every blink of her eyes felt like an eternity between darkness and wakefulness.

One of the men sat against a tree and kept night watch with his rifle perched on his knee. The rest of the men gathered around the fire, along with Red, who plopped down next to Alice for his evening slumber. She tried to inch away from him out of fear and spite, but was too tired to move very far.

As she surrendered to sleep, a gust of wind rustled the trees. The horses neighed and stomped their hooves against the forest floor. Alice was comforted as she thought of her brother, James, and his horse, Chief. She was so glad that James had found an animal friend. *Maybe they are out looking for me now,* she mused. She imagined large search parties with soldiers from Fort Ellis. "More reinforcements!" they would cry. "We must find Alice!" As she drifted off, she imagined parades of men trotting toward her in army uniforms. They would sit on their horses, blowing horns through the grassy plains, looking through binoculars for Alice. Indian trackers would lead them to her.

Alice dozed off, giving in to her relaxing muscles.

Despite her exhaustion, her rest was brief. She kept awakening throughout the night from fear and coughing fits. It had been a few days since her capture, and she had yet to sleep through the night. She would catch glimpses of things in the camp as she drifted in and out of sleep. Some seemed real, some didn't. Her eyes opened, and she saw animal eyes glowing by the light of the fire. She let out a little yelp, and the animal darted away. Then there was darkness. She awoke again to the sounds of Slinger and Farley sitting together sharing a drink. Red was sleeping, huddled under a few blankets. The nights were cold in Yellowstone, even in the summer, and it could rain or even snow at the most unpredictable times. But tonight it was just windy. It was the kind of wind that carried voices in peculiar directions.

"What do ya think, Farley, what do ya think?" Slinger tilted his head back and took a chug of his drink. His long legs jutted up and his knees looked particularly pointy next to Farley's stumpy stature. Alice opened and closed her droopy eyelids.

"I say let's get rid of both of them," Farley stated.

"But I thought you said Red was alright," Slinger whined.

"Maybe, maybe not. They're both kids, and kids are a

useless nuisance. They're just using up our provisions."

"But Red's man enough; I'd feel like I was betrayin' Bloody Knuckles to kill the kid." Slinger looked into the fire with a frown.

"Maybe. But let's take care of the girl tomorrow."

"Well, why don't we just leave them out here in the wilds?" Slinger offered.

"Maybe." Farley took out his freshly sharpened knife and examined it in the fading embers. For a moment, it flashed a reflection of the moon. Alice thought they were looking over in her direction, so she closed her eyes again, pretending to be asleep. In truth, she was wide awake, and her heart was pounding.

"Let's not do anything tomorrow. We'll go one more day and then decide tomorrow night, unless I get an urge during the day. We're only a few sleeps away from the Hole in the Wall. We'll meet up with more guys there, maybe write to G, and then we can decide what to do," Farley spoke slowly.

"Well, we're not bringin' an eleven-year-old girl to the Hole in the Wall. I don't think there's ever been a lady at that hideaway, let alone a little lady. No siree. People will notice and we might get in trouble for it," Slinger squealed in quick, nervous contrast to Farley's heavy speech.

"Maybe you're right," Farley admitted. "But there still might be some money in it if we keep her around. We can always try and renegotiate with G, even though Bloody Knuckles isn't around." Farley stood, hiked up his britches, and then walked heavily to his sleeping place. Slinger followed.

As Alice looked up, she saw Red's eyes wide open, now fearful too. They stared at each other for a long moment in the fading moonlight, the fire smoking next to them.

Chapter 2

RESPONSIBILITY

Dear Miles,

I need your help. It is urgent. We've been looking for Alice every day, but there is no sign of her. Have you heard anything? Is there any way to get more soldiers down from Fort Ellis, or friends from Bozeman to help with the search?

Each morning since Alice's disappearance, hours before dawn, James would awaken to the voice of his stepfather Jed, saying, "James, get your things. Let's go." He would slowly open his eyes and see his mother, Mattie, preparing some food outside the tent, the dark circles around her eyes sinking in deeper with each passing day of his sister's absence. He would gather up his things, and the search for Alice would begin.

I am not sure when we will return to Bozeman. Mother wants to stay nearby and keep searching. ... I wish I knew how to make her feel better; she doesn't look well. We hear that there will be government men arriving any day now to explore the Yellowstone. Is it really going to be Dr. Hayden and the same Geological Survey that explored here last year? Knowing they'll be coming any day now is the only thing that keeps me ...

James paused his writing at the sound of something rustling outside his tent. There was a strange moaning noise. He put his pen down and reached for a rifle. *It must be a large animal,* James thought. The noise got louder and louder and it approached the front of his tent. James was ready.

"MRRRAHHHHH!" his friend Tom jumped around the corner and growled, his hands raised in the air like claws.

"You pea brain! I almost shot you!" James exclaimed.

"MAHHH!" Tom marched forward threateningly, swiping his "claws" through the air.

"Stop it, it's too early." James sat back down. Tom casually became a human again.

"It's never too early to make you feel stupid," Tom said flatly, his dark black hair falling into his eyes.

James always appreciated how his best friend spoke; there wasn't a lot of variety to his tone. James had met Tom when he first moved to Bozeman a year ago, and they quickly became best friends. James invited him to come on their family holiday at Mammoth Hot Springs in the recently established Yellowstone National Park. Little did they know that the trip would end in a dramatic disappearance.

"What are you doing?" Tom asked.

"Writing a letter to Miles," James said. Miles was a gruff newspaperman who wrote for the *Bozeman Avant Courier*. James had promised to be his Yellowstone Correspondent and tell him about their adventures on holiday. Miles was always the first person James thought of when problems came up, and there seemed to be plenty of those recently. Miles was well-connected; he knew a lot of people and a lot about people.

"Well, we'll have new stories to tell him when we find Alice. Look what I've got." Tom threw down a satchel and smiled mischievously at James. "I've packed my bags and I'm ready to go find Alice for real. No more of these 'morning only' searches. Let's go for longer. "

"But it's Sunday and Jed won't approve. He thinks

we should rest and pray," James said, rolling his eyes. James picked up his compass longingly. Tom was about to answer when Jed stepped into the tent. Both of the boys stood up abruptly and James put the compass behind his back.

"Good morning, Reverend," Tom said plainly, stepping in front of his bag.

"Why, good morning, Tom," Jed replied.

"Good morning," James said. "I thought you went out for an early hunt."

"No, I just went for a short walk around the hot spring terraces. What a marvel. The colors are so magnificent—the oranges and blues. In the morning, the steam is especially strong against the cool air." Jed looked down and saw Tom's packed excursion bag. Then he noticed James fidgeting.

"What do you have behind your back?" Jed asked.

"Oh, nothing. Just the compass," James replied, turning red and nervously bringing the compass from behind his back. The small tent suddenly became silent and uncomfortable.

"Hmmm … is that breakfast I smell outside?" Tom changed the subject and figured out how to get himself out of the tent. "Smells delicious. I'm going to go and see."

"That's a good idea, Tom," Jed said, deep in thought.

Tom picked up his bag and exited the tent, glancing at James as he departed.

"James, let's go and collect some firewood," Jed said. James put the compass down and put aside his letter to Miles to finish later. Jed put his arm around James' shoulder and escorted him out of the tent.

James felt his stomach rumble and wished he had been sent to breakfast instead. They walked outside of camp and away from the hot springs into denser woods.

Mornings were cold in the mountains, and James could see his breath. It was the middle of the summer, but sometimes there was even frost. James rubbed his hands together. He looked back and saw the steam rising up from the incredible cascades and terraces of Mammoth Hot Springs, just as Jed had described. They had been forming for thousands of years, tenaciously boiling up to the surface and depositing their special magic onto the earth. James looked back at the small encampment, at the large formation called Liberty Cap, and at the rudimentary bathhouses that had been built to attract new tourists. James was acutely aware of Jed's weighty presence. He couldn't suppress the feeling that somehow he was in trouble. *I hope we make this firewood collection quick,* James thought uncomfortably.

Some of the trees near the springs were petrified, like the one at Tom and James' secret meeting spot, so they couldn't use those trees for wood—they were part rock! James had learned that trees became petrified and stony when they filled with minerals over a long period of time. It always amazed him that he was standing on an active volcano, and scenes like the petrified forest were constant reminders.

They walked along in awkward silence for a while. When they finally made it up to a healthy forest and walked past perfect firewood, James quickly realized that he and Jed probably weren't going to collect anything at all.

"Look at that, I think you grew an inch since you came to Bozeman last year." Jed let out a clumsy laugh and James tried not to roll his eyes. He felt the impending doom of a conversation that he didn't want to have. He wondered how he would have felt walking in the woods right now with his real father. "James, I can see that you're not just a boy anymore, you're a young man. And I am going to have to ask you to do something as a man."

Suddenly, James felt his sense of importance swell. *What could I do to prove myself?* James began to hope that his stepfather would recognize that James was grown up enough to do what he had already secretly planned to do with Tom—go off on their own to look for Alice.

"I spoke with your mother last night and she is very upset about your sister. I know you are, too, and you've been shouldering it very well. I pray every day that God is watching over her. I hope you do, too."

James didn't answer. He didn't really connect with prayer in the way that the preacher or his sister did. It always seemed to him that actually doing something was more important than praying for it to happen.

"I need to ask you a favor. I get a sense that you and Tom are going to try and find Alice yourselves."

James could see that the preacher had started to break out into his typical nervous sweat. Any time Jed was having a serious talk with James, his upper lip began to bead with perspiration.

"I am going to ask that you and Tom do not try and find her on your own."

James' heart sank.

"But I need you to know why—because I think

your efforts are most noble and all good young men should go out to do what they think is right. In this case, I am thinking of your mother. It is dangerous out here in the wild. It would break your mother's heart if something happened to you. I need you to be a man and be responsible by staying by her side. And I've decided that we must go back to Bozeman."

"No!" James blurted out. He couldn't stop the words from angrily spilling out. "We can't leave Yellowstone. What if Alice comes back and we're not here? Does Mother know about this decision?"

The preacher had removed his arm from James' shoulder. James' voice became louder and louder. "We need to do *more,* not less. Day excursions aren't enough anymore; she may have gone farther away by this point."

"James, they have soldiers out looking for her. We've gone every morning. We don't want men to have to look for us next for being foolhardy."

James tightened his fists in frustration. He was so angry with his stepfather for putting him in this position. *It was not foolhardy to search for Alice!* Jed continued walking in silence and James tried to breathe and think for a moment. As much as he hated it, the more he thought about it, the more he understood what Jed was saying. He had to be responsible and he knew it. His mother did seem sickly and out of sorts lately. Mattie kept excusing herself from conversations to go lie down. Sometimes he would see her leaning against a tree or a boulder for support. If she was willing to leave Yellowstone, there was nothing he could do.

"I understand," James finally responded. His fists remained clenched as they turned around and headed back to camp.

~ *Chapter 3* ~

FIRE

The next morning, Alice awoke to Red forcefully shaking her shoulders. She coughed as smoke filled her lungs and the smell of burning wood seared her nostrils. Opening her eyes through a haze of ash-filled smoke, she saw chaos all around her. Horses were bucking in the air, pots and pans were clanking to the ground, and branches were crumbling off the trees. Men's shouts filled the thick air. The fire had engulfed their whole campsite.

"Get out of my way!" Farley careened past her. His hair was singed and the side of his body was blazing. Alice looked around and saw that the wind had picked up even more from the night before, sending the night's dying embers into a raging forest fire. Alice's feet and hands were still tied together, so she tried to roll backward, away from the flames.

"Hold still," Red growled, jerking her back. He pulled out a knife from his pocket and sawed through the ropes. The heat from the flames was making Alice feel faint. Her fragile lungs gasped for air.

"Over here!" a gang member shouted. His horse pulled on its reins, trying to escape the blaze. Through the thickening smoke, Alice could see the henchmen starting to catch their fleeing horses and assemble.

"Head south, head south!" another shouted. The sounds of the fire surrounded Alice, and the world started moving in slow motion. Red untied her, but the shouting, the horses, the smoke, and the crackling trees began overwhelming her senses and lulling her back into unconsciousness. Suddenly, a large, decrepit tree that had been burning snapped right beside them and came crashing to the ground.

"Look out!" Alice shouted. Jolted back into lucidity, she tackled Red to the ground to avoid the crush of the plummeting old trunk. They paused for a moment, thankful for escaping death or severe injury by only a few inches. Ash puffed up from the simmering earth, and burned Alice's eyes.

"Come on," Red said, standing up and snatching his knife. He yanked her arm and pulled her toward the rest of the group.

His grip on her arm quickly brought her back to the reality of the fire. *Maybe this is my chance,* she thought to herself. She remembered the terrible conversation she had overheard between Farley and Slinger, and the image of their devil faces dancing by the fire. She recalled the threat of her throat being cut, and pictured herself bleeding to death in the woods. *What would my family do if they found me dead like that?* Alice gained strength at the thought of her family, and she hit the knife out of Red's hand. He fell back, startled by her sudden energy. She bent down to pick it up and held it up to Red amidst the mayhem of horses braying, men running, and smoke rising.

"I'm not going back with them." Her voice was firm and confident, despite the madness of the blaze and the pain in her lungs. Red said nothing, the knife up to his throat. He was completely startled by Alice's force. Their eyes met through the smoke, and through Red's icy stare, Alice felt a moment of recognition about the ominous conversation they had heard the night before. Sensing that he would not stop her, she lowered the knife to focus on her escape route.

Alice turned to head in the opposite direction, but a wall of fire blocked her way. She quickly scanned the scene and saw a small path between two sections of the fire. It was closing fast, the flames jumping quickly and merrily between the trees. The henchmen were distractedly calming their horses and salvaging any goods they could.

Alice felt like a character in an adventure and tried to figure out what a storybook hero would do. She picked up the blanket she had used for sleep and wrapped herself in it. Red was still standing in place, paralyzed.

"What are they doing over there?" Alice heard Farley's booming voice shout. "Red, get a move on!"

Ready ...

Red seemed to hesitate before responding to Farley's call.

Set ...

"Red, get that girl and come on! Pick up the gunny sack!"

Go!

Alice darted through the enclosing fire. She could barely see beyond the smoke. She lifted her hands up and used the blanket as a shield.

"She's getting away!" Slinger squealed. His horse neighed and bucked.

"Forget it. Let her burn! Come on!" Alice heard Farley say, but it sounded as if his voice were coming through a long, narrow tube. The burning of the trees grew louder than anything she could have imagined. *It's like the trees are screaming for their lives,* she thought to herself. The smoke was so heavy, she couldn't see where she was going any more. Her foot got caught on a fallen log and she stumbled to the ground. Instinctively, she rolled with the momentum of her fall and quickly scrambled to her feet. She coughed and pulled the blanket tighter.

You can make it, she reassured herself. Alice could feel the tightness in her chest with every inhalation of air. She felt like someone was squeezing her windpipe. Her eyes burned so intensely that she had to close them and blindly charge forward.

Don't stop, don't stop. She struggled onward. Finally, Alice felt a clean burst of air. She opened her eyes and looked up to see thick smoke billowing up into the sky. *Did I make it?* she wondered. Dropping the blanket, Alice's knees buckled underneath her and her small body fell to the ground with a thud. She sank deep into unconsciousness.

~ *Chapter 4* ~

THE HAYDEN EXPEDITION

James returned to camp anxious to find Tom and tell him the troubling news: rather than search for Alice, they would soon be leaving the park altogether. As he walked around, he surveyed what Mr. McCartney and Mr. Horr, the founders of the shack-hotel, had built in their short time at Yellowstone. There were about thirty people in the camp at Mammoth Hot Springs now, and a few small houses and baths had been erected. James was proud that he had helped McCartney and Horr realize the dreams of their fledgling business. The hotel was the only official accommodation in all of Yellowstone. McCartney and Horr sent numerous documents back and forth to the government trying to ensure that their little place would be a legitimate landmark in the park in the years to come. Getting to the springs from a civilized outpost was a long, bumpy, and dirty toil. But despite the isolated location, there seemed to be plenty of people enjoying the scenery and bathing in the waters. James thought this showed promise.

Many of the travelers who had come down from Bozeman in James' original party had already departed. Railroad man Aldous Kruthers and his family had set out to return to Virginia. After Alice had disappeared, Kruthers said he felt the holiday was over, and James knew what he meant. In parting, Kruthers kindly remarked that he was sure he would see James again, given James' thirst for the railroads and politics.

Even though he missed the Bozeman families, James was fond of the new people that had arrived. One of them was particularly exciting to him: a photographer named Joshua Crissman. He and his wife had recently moved to Bozeman with their daughter, Elizabeth. They accompanied him on the trip down to the springs.

On his way to find Tom, James saw Crissman taking photographs of some of the new tourists from Virginia

City. Crissman's hair was slicked back around his flat, square face, and his eyes were wide-set. His bushy goatee and moustache extended at least two inches below his chin, completely consuming his mouth in a layer of thick, straggly strands. When his mouth was closed, it was impossible to tell if he even had lips. This seemed fitting, given his mild manner and quiet demeanor. But he came vivaciously alive when he was taking pictures.

Crissman's daughter Elizabeth helped her father by posing his subjects with their hands in their laps or gallantly placed on their hips. Elizabeth looked to be about thirteen, like James. She was petite with long, curly brown hair and eyes that reminded James of a sweet puppy's gaze. The Crissmans had just arrived at camp a few days earlier, and Elizabeth was as quiet as her father. James noticed that her fingernails were raw from biting. He often saw her mother pull the girl's hand away from her mouth to stop her from gnawing on herself.

On this day, Crissman was photographing four men and a woman. The lady was clad in a full, dark dress from her neck to her ankles to protect her skin from the sun, remain proper, and conceal dirt and stains. James looked off to the side at Elizabeth as he passed by the scene. *I wonder what I would say to her,* he thought. Suddenly, he bumped head-on into a man.

"Excuse me!" James said.

"Oof. I'm sorry," the man said, scrambling. His notebook slipped and a paper fluttered to the ground.

"No, I'm sorry. I wasn't looking where I was going," James politely apologized.

"I wasn't really either. You can't walk around with your head buried in notes, or it ends up like this," the man said, his skinny fingers reorganizing his work. James noticed the man's well-worn boots and saw numbers and measurements on the stray paper as he bent to pick it up. The man lifted his hat and ran his fingers through his light, graying hair and smiled.

"I'm sorry again. I am just making my way over to greet Mr. Crissman over there taking photographs. My name is Dr. Hayden."

James gulped. *Dr. Hayden. Dr. Hayden. Dr. Ferdinand Vandeveer Hayden.* He knew that name backward and forward. He looked up at the man's thin face and into his squinty eyes with disbelief. James and his family had read Hayden's annual survey report before they had even moved out West. He was the head of the whole government expedition in 1871 that helped create Yellowstone as a national park! And now the famous Hayden Expedition had arrived in Yellowstone at the same time he was there! James had never been in awe of any man other than his father, but this man was a hero. He wanted to embrace Dr. Hayden, but decided that would be improper and odd.

"I'm James," he finally mustered up the courage to say. *Dr. Hayden himself! I can't wait to tell Tom.* James' mind raced wildly. *He's not as tall as I imagined. And look at how light his beard and moustache are and how his ears stick out!*

"Hello, James. Pleased to make your acquaintance. Where are you here from, if I may ask?"

"Bozeman, now, I suppose. We moved here last year to be with my stepfather who is a preacher, and my sister is lost, and my mother is sad, but I am really glad you are here." *Stop talking!* he thought to himself. *Why am I rambling on like this?* "But I'm originally from New York."

"New York?" Dr. Hayden looked pleasantly surprised. "Any prominent relations I may know of?"

James put on his best airs. "I think my father had several connections in Congress and my family does have quite a lot of influence. In fact, I am just writing a letter to my uncle, Senator McCormick, right now." *I think he's a senator,* James thought. *I know my father's sister married him and I think he works in government. . . .*

"We'll have to keep that in mind," Hayden said. "We're looking for a few more local assistants to help with hauling and packing."

"Indeed." James pulled himself together, trying to sound sophisticated. A plan was starting to hatch in James' mind.

"How old are you?" Hayden inquired.

"Sixteen," James blurted.

"Really?" Hayden said.

"Well, in a little while I will be . . ." He didn't know how to stop his lie. "Is Mr. William Henry Jackson here, too?" James couldn't conceal his excitement. "I have seen lots of his photographs, and Mr. Crissman's photos as well. A lot of people say that it was because of your advertisements of the park and because of the work of Mr. Jackson and the artist Thomas Moran. . . . Oh, is he here?"

"No, sadly he had other obligations this year," Hayden chuckled, warmed by James' enthusiasm.

"Well, it is because of your work last year that the

park even exists at all. So I just want to say . . ." *What do I want to say? What do I want to say?* James had no idea.

"So I just want to say ... congratulations!" He exclaimed. *Congratulations? I sound like a real idiot.* James blushed. Luckily, Dr. Hayden didn't seem to mind James' comments.

"Well, thank you. You've certainly got a fine mind and you've definitely done your research. To answer an earlier question, unfortunately the photographer Mr. Jackson was not able to travel with us for this part of the expedition. In fact, that is why I'm heading over to talk to Mr. Crissman, so we can use his services."

"Oh, well, that's mighty stupendous," James said.

"Mr. Jackson is coming up from the south with an additional group, the Snake River Division. They will be studying the Grand Teton mountain range."

"Wow!" James gushed. "I mean, that's most interesting," he said, trying to tone down his enthusiasm and deepen his voice. James had heard of these amazing mountain peaks and wished he could see them. The Tetons were outside of Yellowstone's southern border, many miles away, so that fantasy didn't seem likely to come true any time soon. But he was very interested in every aspect of Hayden's work for the U.S. government.

James felt questions pile up in the front of his head like a horse stampede. *What do you think of Yellowstone? Have you discovered anything new? What do the geysers look like? Will you take me to find my sister? Can the government stop people from killing all of the animals? Can the government protect the natural wonders from tourists and vandals?*

"Well, I hope you enjoy your stay," was all James managed to pull out of his brain. Not even a question at all. As he turned from Hayden, James saw that a whole brigade of government men had arrived at the hot springs. They were Hayden's hand-picked entourage. Accompanying the group were about forty mules; each of them looked like a traveling general store, with instruments and pots attached to its back. The group had started its expedition months before, so it was visibly worn already. There were cartographers, geologists, general assistants, painters, cooks, hunters, guides, and mineralogists. James' head was spinning with the excitement of the new arrivals.

"That's only half of them," Tom said, walking up to James, who stood with his mouth agape.

"Tom!" James exclaimed. "This is amazing!"

"The other half of the Hayden Expedition is coming

into the park from the south through the Tetons."

"I know," James said confidently.

"Did you know that the new superintendent of Yellowstone National Park, Langford, is actually with them?" Tom looked at James.

"Wow," James said. *The superintendent himself! The man who would take care of the park!*

"I knew that part would make you happy," Tom said. It did, but part of James was disappointed that he didn't get to speak to this superintendent in person.

"I've been taking notes," Tom continued. He was also drinking some sort of berry juice. "I already had a great conversation with Dr. Peale, the mineralogist. He wants to keep me as his son!"

"Really?" James looked at Tom with awe.

"No. But I almost offered it myself."

"Good. I was going to say, your mother is probably never going to let you go anywhere with my family ever again because we've kept you out here at the hot springs for so long."

"Ha. She's fine. My brothers are keeping her busy, I'm sure. She loves the socials anyway. She writes me mighty long letters full of boring retellings of who said what in town." Tom's mouth was turning red from his drink. His berry-stained mouth made his skin look even whiter against his ink-colored hair.

"Listen to some of these excellent horse names they have on the expedition." Tom flipped back a page and started reading a list. "There's Old Mortality, Cyclops, Rustler, Sowbelly, Canalboat, Guts, Pot Gut—um ... Oh, I love this ... they sometimes call him Tub-O-Gut. And they even have one named Alice!"

"I know she likes animals, but I'm not sure she'd want a horse named after her," James said.

"We'll have to ask her ourselves."

It was the first time that James had felt lighthearted in days. He loved that his closest friend still felt so confident that Alice was alive. It made all the difference in the world.

"I am going to talk to Dr. Peale and Dr. Hayden about all the possible medicinal properties in Yellowstone to figure out a cure for Alice's cough, too," Tom said.

"They just got here. How many people could you have spoken to already?" James asked, amazed. James realized that the only person who could possibly be more excited than he was by the arrival of the government's Hayden Expedition was Tom.

"I've spoken to most of the important ones—the

doctors and scientists. I am on my way to do some readings of the springs with the scientists and ask them more about last year's findings. They're just starting now, and they'll do great things, I can tell." Not even Tom's monotonous voice could conceal his excitement. "Want to come?"

"I think I better check in with my mother first, see how she's doing with all the new arrivals."

"Okay," Tom rambled on. "I'm sure these hot springs and other curiosities have ways of curing people, too, but most of the scientists don't think that sitting in them does much, or that breathing in their fumes is really helpful. They actually think it might be toxic in some cases."

"Well, that's reassuring."

"I know," Tom said, "but I am not convinced that Alice really has consumption. You said she's always had trouble breathing, since she was real little, right?"

"Yes," James answered, unsure of how this made the situation better.

"So, she is probably just an asthmatic," Tom theorized. "Many people have asthma and they live a long time." This was the most he had ever heard Tom talk. *Maybe he won't be a geologist after all, but a doctor,*

James wondered. *The best way to become a natural scientist these days is to become a doctor first, anyway. Just like Dr. Hayden.*

"Anyway," Tom continued, "are you keeping busy figuring out how to protect all the people, animals, and my favorite wonders?"

"Yes. No. I don't know." James, Tom, and Alice had made a pact to protect the wilderness of the park and its animals after seeing how and why the buffalo were being grossly over-hunted. The pledge was the culmination of their commitment to each other and their natural surroundings. They had gathered at the secret meeting spot and collectively stated their promises, then tore a piece of fabric off their clothes and tied it to their wrists as a symbol of their unity and dedication. James glanced at his wristband. When the three of them were together, he had felt powerful, and he knew they would make a difference for the park and the animals. But with Alice gone ... James didn't have the heart to carry on with their pledge anymore. He felt lost.

"You'll figure something out. I'm here if you need me." Tom held up his arm with the wristband and lifted the corner of his mouth in a half smile. Tom knew just how to rekindle his friend's hope and commitment. James gave a half smile back and lifted up his own arm to show his wristband, the emblem of their pact.

"Okay, I'll see you later. Hopefully my notebook will be full by then. Oh, and what did Jed say to you?"

James looked at Tom's beaming face and didn't have the heart to tell him that they would soon be leaving Mammoth Hot Springs, their grand plans for finding Alice denied.

"Nothing," he fibbed. *Maybe there's another way to safely look for Alice,* James considered. *No need to get discouraged yet,* he thought, the seeds of a plan growing in his mind.

James finally made it back to the tent to see his mother. He was lost in thought—about Alice, about the government expedition, and about his forced return to Bozeman. As he got closer, he heard raised, tense voices coming from inside. He quietly stepped forward to eavesdrop.

"It's still early, I'll be fine," he heard his mother say.

"No, we're going back," Jed answered nervously. James could imagine the drops of sweat collecting on his stepfather's lip.

"There are doctors here. I'll be fine," Mattie responded.

"I am aware of the doctors," Jed said sternly. "In fact, I spoke to one and he agrees that you should go back to Bozeman."

"What did you say to him?"

"I already requested that he come to examine you later this afternoon, following this discussion."

James' stomach turned. *Is Mother sick?* he wondered nervously.

Mattie was silent.

"Mattie. Please. You are so important to me. This . . . this is so important to me."

"I'm sorry, but my daughter is important to me. You are just being selfish! You are thinking of your own child!" she said with uncharacteristic anger.

His own child?

"That is preposterous and insulting, Madeleine. I've looked for Alice with all of the strength that God has given me. I've done nothing but care for this family," he argued defensively. "I even descended into this wretched, hellish wilderness for her."

"It hasn't been long enough! I'm not going back to Bozeman. She's still out there. I can feel it." Suddenly James heard the sound of something crash and fall to the floor.

"Mattie! Sit down. Drink this. I'm going to call on the doctor immediately. Are you okay? Stay with me." James nervously clutched the side of the tent and almost ran to get a doctor himself when he heard his mother's voice again.

"I'm sorry ... don't go," she said meekly. "I'm okay. I'm sorry I was cross."

"Oh, Mattie. Please forgive me for losing my temper." Jed's voice was shaking.

"Just hold me," she said weakly. There was a moment of quiet.

"Mattie, this is it. I've decided. We're going back and that's final. Alice is in the hands of Providence. Patterson and the troops out from Fort Ellis will continue to search for her. But we have to think of the future. We have to think of your health and the baby's health."

The baby?! James almost let out a gasp. *Well, this changes everything.*

"What if I travel and lose it then? It's not an easy journey," she said, her confidence waning.

"Better to go back to Bozeman sooner than later, Mattie; it's just going to get harder."

James heard the sounds of crying.

"Oh, Jed. I feel so lost."

~ *Chapter 5* ~
ALONE

Alice lay still, beginning to regain consciousness. She remembered running through the fire and seeing a sliver of white sky before everything went dark. *But where am I now?* she wondered. Her body felt stiff. She heard a methodical snapping next to her as she struggled to open her eyes. *Is someone walking toward me?* she considered. Then she took a sharp breath in and smelled something strong, intoxicating, sweet. The aroma helped her focus, and she saw a young man's back bent over. She heard the snapping sounds again. *Could it be my brother?*

"James?" she said.

"No, it's Red." He turned around and revealed his

scarred lip and freckled face. He stood next to a pile of twigs.

Alice quickly tried to sit up and a small vial fell over on her chest and spilled.

"What was that?" she questioned nervously, pushing off the vial. The liquid rolled down her arm.

"To wake you up. It has a strong smell." There was a pause and Red went back to splitting the branches into smaller pieces. The sound of a strange bird and a rattling noise sent both of their eyes up, looking for danger.

"Where are we? Where is the rest of the gang?" Alice quickly looked around, distrusting.

"Not here." Red turned and kept breaking the branches in half. It was quiet. Alice looked down and saw that she was still wrapped in her blanket. Both she and Red were dark and sooty from the fire. Their faces were filthy and their shoes looked slightly charred.

"What are you doing?"

"Breaking up branches to start a fire."

"Are we alone?" Alice asked.

"You ask a lot of questions."

"And you don't have enough answers!" Alice was furious. *What a brat,* she thought to herself. "Where are we? How and why are we here? Are people looking ..."

"You're horribly annoying."

"So are you. Answer me!"

"Well, you ran through a fire, and I followed you. I don't think that Slinger and Farley will be looking for us. I think they're happy to leave us to the bears."

Alice sat up further. "Why did you follow me?"

"I didn't think you would survive alone. I doubt we'll survive together, but I figured we had a better chance with matches, sugar, a little food, a gun, and a sharp knife."

"And how did we get ... here?" They were under a tree, sitting above a marshy area on top of a large, jutting volcanic rock.

"I carried you."

Alice's face burned like the fire.

"You fainted just past the fire, but it was spreading fast so we had to move. It's still flaming." Alice looked to where Red nodded his head and saw a mass of smoke in the distance.

"That's a mile away!" She coughed.

"You're not that heavy," he said. It was quiet for a long while. Alice was unsure of how to respond to this gesture from Red. She still didn't trust him, but maybe he wasn't as evil as she had thought. And he had probably saved her life. As he returned to his branch snapping, Alice examined their surroundings. Nearby, she saw a gushing waterfall.

"That's beautiful!" she exclaimed.

"Yes," he agreed, catching himself before he could smile at her. "And don't get the wrong idea. I think you're silly and that your brother is a snot, and this is probably the last place on Earth I'd like to be."

"Well, thanks for making that clear!" Alice folded her arms.

"You're welcome." Red went over to some kindling

he had assembled, and used a match to start a fire. He blew into the center of his stick pile, nurturing the flame. He was protective of his few matches.

"I shot us a marmot to eat," Red announced, pointing to a limp animal in the dirt.

Alice's face twisted in disgust. "I'm sure you shot whatever else you could set your bloody eyes on, too."

"What do you know about that?" Red said in a quick, harsh, and terrifying voice. It was like he was suppressing a turbulent sea of dark secrets. Alice winced a little at his icy blue eyes.

"Nothing."

"Anyway, I was too busy carrying you to do much of anything. It's pretty darn lucky we got this. It's a meal fit for a princess, so it should be good enough for you," he said snidely.

"I said thank you."

"No, you didn't."

"Well, THANK YOU!" Alice stood up and walked over to look at the waterfall. She tried to orient herself. *How can I get out of here and away from Red,* she thought with a shudder.

Alice looked at where the sun was positioned. She had been keeping track of where the gang had taken her and could tell they were heading east. She figured they were taking the Bannock Trail, a known Indian trail in the park. *It's a good thing James, Tom, and I looked at all the maps in Miles' office,* Alice thought. She sighed, rubbing her wrists where the tied ropes had chafed her skin. Then she looked down at her wristband. It was tattered, but still intact. It seemed like a lifetime ago that she had pledged with her brother and Tom to protect animals and the wilderness. When they had been together, she felt indestructible. Now she was lost in the wilderness with animals all about, and she was the one that needed protection.

Red looked over and saw her examining the wristband. A gust of cold wind promised a change of weather.

"It looks like it's going to rain," Alice said, trying to be brave and helpful.

"Or hail. These mountains are unpredictable."

"We should probably stay here for the night."

Red nodded in agreement and they looked at each other awkwardly. Suddenly, all of the noises and dangers of the wild were upon Alice. She could feel the glassy eyes of predators around her. *The animals are my friends,* she thought to herself to soothe her nerves. *I just need to stay calm and remember that. I need to listen to what they are saying.* But she didn't hear anything reassuring. All she felt was goose flesh on her arms.

Even though moments earlier she had wanted to poke his eye out with a stick, Alice was suddenly overcome with gratitude for Red's presence. She moved a little closer to the growing fire and shuddered at the frightening hopelessness of their situation: two children in Yellowstone. *Even legendary, grizzled mountain men don't survive out here,* she thought anxiously. The vastness of the danger ahead settled in Alice's stomach and caused even more pain than her growing hunger. *This park is an enormous wilderness,* Alice thought. *We may never be found.*

Chapter 6

THE CHOICE

James found Tom at their secret meeting spot by the gnarled tree. He couldn't wait to tell Tom the news and his new plan. *I can't believe I lied to Dr. Hayden about my age so quickly,* James thought proudly. *It's like I somehow I knew it would pan out for the best.* Tom's science diary was filling up rapidly, and he told James everything that he had notated before James could even get a word in.

"I've made a list of everyone who is on the expedition—well, at least of the important people. I think there's about twenty-five people total, and I have about ten missing, who are just the packers and some of the guides from Fort Ellis."

That seems unfair, James thought. *They're probably the ones who actually know how to do everything.*

"Northern Division" of the Hayden Expedition, U.S. Geological Survey of the Territories

Dr. Ferdinand V. Hayden, Geologist, ● head of it all.

Dr. A. C. Peale, Mineralogist ⊛

Joshua Crissman, Guest Photographer ⊛

A. E. Bingham, Asst. Photographer

W. H. Holmes, Artist

Adolf Burek, Chief Topographer.

A. E. Brown, Asst. Topographer.

E. B. Wakefield, Meteorologist

Walter B. Platt, Naturalist

W. B. Logan, Secretary

Joseph Savage, General Asst.

J. O. C. Sloane, General Asst.

Henry Gannett, Astronomer

Bill (Billy) Hamilton, Old Trapper and Guide ⊛ Killed 600-700 bears, at least

William H. Blackmore, Guest from Britain. ⊛

"Why did you put the artists at the top? I thought you would put all the scientists first," James asked.

"Elizabeth convinced me that the artists are just as important, especially in showing people how amazing the park is. But really, I probably shouldn't have listened to her. It is a geological survey, after all. I don't think Mr. Crissman even appears in the official reports," Tom answered. "At least that's what I heard."

"You've been talking to Elizabeth?" James asked.

"Yes," Tom stated plainly.

"What do you talk about?"

"Not much," Tom answered.

"Oh."

"Why?"

"Just curious."

"Do you fancy her?"

"What? No. I haven't even talked to her," James admitted.

It was quiet for a moment. Then Tom looked up at James and started chanting, "James has a lady friend! James has a lady friend!"

"I do not, dung face."

"James has a lady friend! James has a lady friend!"

"Stop it or I'll smack you," James threatened, his

fists tightening in anger. He lunged at Tom full force, but Tom just stepped out of the way.

"Whoa, you shouldn't let things get to you like that. Elizabeth wouldn't like it!" Tom teased James and smirked.

James collected himself and responded, "Anyway, I haven't even spoken to her, so it's not anything to me. And give me that list."

Tom handed over the diary with the list of the members of the Geological Survey. James looked at it carefully then said, "You're missing two."

Tom took it and looked it over again.

"What do you mean? Where?"

"You need to add James Clifton and Tom Blakely."

"Um, what?" Tom said. "Us? Have you gone to a special fantasy world?"

"I've figured out how we can look for Alice. I spoke to Dr. Hayden and he's looking for a few new general assistants. We just convince him that we're both sixteen, that you are a scientist in training, that I am related to Congressman McCormick, and we're both strong from living out in the country. I'll tell him our true purpose is to join a larger group to find Alice, and he will surely see this as noble. He almost offered me the job on the spot."

Tom looked blankly at James.

"So? Will you come?" James asked nervously.

"What kind of a question is that? Of course I will! The hope of finding Alice and being around a group of scientists?" Tom howled like a wolf in excitement and James followed suit. Then, just as suddenly, a cloud came over Tom's face. "How will I tell my mother? Wait, have you told your mother and Reverend Lawson?"

"Well, that's the tricky part. No." James replied. "There are some other things going on, too ..."

"What are you going to do?"

"I don't know."

The friends headed back to camp filled with a mixture of worry and hope. As they reached the family tent, James quietly crept to his featherbed and fell asleep quickly, despite his many concerns about his mother's health, his secret plan, and Alice's whereabouts.

That night, James had a dream. He was lost in the middle of a geyser field on a moonless night. He felt energy churning under the thin layer of earth's crust, threatening to burst at any moment like a dozen land mines. He couldn't make one false step.

He looked down at his brass compass for guidance, but the needle was spinning around crazily in circles.

He shook it, but it was no help. "Come on," he urgently pleaded with the compass. "I need to know which way to go. Show me which way to go." But the compass needle just accelerated until the compass itself spun out of James' hand and exploded.

He heard a sickening gurgle sound behind him, and the splattering of liquid. Two men bubbled up from inside the geysers. They were covered in mucus, like newborn babies coming fresh from the underworld. The men ripped through their oozing geyser membranes and began wobbling after James, wiping the putrid slime from their eyes.

"We'll get you!" the two watery voices cried from behind him. They started chasing him slowly, but got faster and faster.

Up ahead, far in the woods, James saw a mountain sheep and it shouted from the trees, "Come to me!" And so he did. He ran as fast as he could to the mountain sheep, but the men behind him were getting closer and closer, and the geyser crust was getting thinner and thinner. Geysers started exploding one by one as he darted past, their sulfuric mists spraying him in the eyes. The gooey geyser men plodded forward at full force. "Come to me!" The mountain sheep beckoned again, its huge horns curling around its head.

James woke up coughing. He threw off his blanket and buffalo robe to let the frigid mountain air hit his skin. The sounds of the night owls and coyotes filled his ears, happily replacing the geyser explosions from his nightmare. He quickly threw on clothes and reread the note that he had written for Mattie and Jed. *I don't know if this is the best way to tell them my plan to search for Alice, but I can't think of any other way,* he thought to himself. In the beginning of the letter, James confessed that he knew about the baby, and then he described the expedition plans in detail so his mother wouldn't worry. By the time he reread the end, his hand was shaking. "Please do not come after me, I beg of you. I am a man, not a boy. Tom and I were accepted to go. It is the perfect solution. I will be well-protected while we search all of Yellowstone for Alice, and you can go back home. We may save Alice's life. I will see you back in Bozeman, and I will write to you. Please make sure Tom's mom knows too. He promises to write also." He scanned the note one final time and signed his name at the bottom.

He hoped he was doing the right thing.

~ *Chapter 7* ~

LOST

Alice and Red passed the day in terror. Hail pelted them torturously. As night fell and the storm passed overhead, both real and imagined beasts seemed to be staring at them. Alice and Red huddled together next to the withering fire. With every rustle in the brush, Red would ready his gun. He even shot a few times into the distance hoping a search party would hear them.

When Alice and Red woke up in the morning and found themselves snuggled up next to each other, they quickly separated. They were tired, wet, dirty, and hungry. The unlikely pair wandered wearily down the side of the cliff, the horror of their situation weighing on them. They meandered for hours in what seemed to be circles, until they resigned themselves to the fact that they were lost. The deer, elk, and mountain sheep stared at Alice and Red, more surprised than fearful that these two young people were among them.

They sat down next to a small trickling stream, exhausted. They drank thirstily and Red filled his canteen. He took out an assembly of goods from his bag and washed his face in the stream. Alice saw a bottle of whiskey among his belongings. She remembered Red's father, Bloody Knuckles, and how rowdy he and his gang became at night.

"What's that for?" Alice asked.

"Not what you're thinking," Red stated.

"How do you know what I'm thinking?"

"Because I can see through you," Red claimed. Alice was taken aback. *What did he mean by that?* she thought, then shuddered. *He's not only scary, he's creepy.* But she was determined to stay calm.

"I think we're lost," Alice said.

"Yes," Red replied.

"And I am starving. Is there any way we could find something to eat?" Red put on a little smirk that Alice really, really hated. He lifted the barrel in his rifle and spun it.

"I don't have many bullets left."

Alice's stomach growled.

"We wasted too many bullets last night," Alice said.

"You didn't think that at the time," Red retorted.

"Yes, I did. You were shooting at nothing."

"Well, you were shivering on me."

Oooooh! She hated him so much.

"You were scared, too!" she pointed out.

"Anyway, I want to save some ammunition in case we come across Indians."

"I wish there was some way to leave clues as to where we are. I am sure that James, Mother, and Jed are looking for me—probably with a whole troop. Maybe if we leave things behind ..." She reached down and tore a piece from the sash of her frayed cotton dress. She took the fabric and pierced it on a tree branch.

"No one is going to find that," Red said skeptically.

"I'm sure they have scouts. Maybe I'll keep leaving pieces wherever we go."

"Then you won't have a dress anymore."

"Enough! You ... you ... ugh," she stammered in frustration. "At least I'm trying something." She coughed dramatically. But she decided that Red was right and that leaving little pieces of cloth everywhere would probably amount to nothing.

"Well, maybe if we find our way back onto the Bannock Trail ..." Red suggested, trailing off hopelessly.

Alice was starting to feel delirious with hunger again, and her sides were sore from coughing through the night. She and Red got up and walked aimlessly, trying to find a path or trail. But it was no use; the surroundings looked the same. Grass, sagebrush, trees, marsh, birds, strange calls, howls, hisses. Alice felt like everything was trying to talk to her all at once, and all too quickly. She had to cover her ears for a moment to escape the noises.

They wandered for a few more hours, hoping to find some semblance of a trail. They had even tried to retrace their steps back to where the now-settled fire had raged. They had hoped to find their old camp and see if any other provisions were left behind, but they could not make sense of the burnt section of the forest.

Finally, they sat to rest for a while. As they huddled, holding their knees to their chests for warmth, Alice saw a plant so bright in color that it stood out against all of the deep pines. It almost called to her in her

hungry and delirious state. She stood up from their resting place and wobbled over on weak legs. She pulled the plant out by its root. The root was shaped like a radish. She quickly tasted it, and it was good! Alice was so ravenous that she devoured the whole thing and went searching for another.

Then she remembered her irritating companion who had carried her away from the fire and fed her marmot meat. She stood up and went over to him.

"I think I found us something to eat," she said, holding up the radish-shaped meal.

"Alice, you can't just eat any old root. Some of them are poisonous!"

"But it tastes good!" Alice shamefully responded.

Red sat forward and examined the plant, then tasted it.

"I think this is thistle root, which luckily we can eat," he said. He stood up and went over to gather more plants.

"This is good. This is good!" he said, overjoyed. They both laughed at the happiness of finding more food. It was food they could take with them, to keep them going until someone found them. In this moment, Alice was delighted that she had a companion, even if it was one that she couldn't stand. The more she thought about it, the more she realized how much Red had risked for her since her capture.

I wonder whose side he's really on, she thought to herself. *He knows all of his father's secrets.* Alice still didn't trust him.

"Don't eat any more or you'll be sick," Red warned, watching her try to devour another root. She put it down, annoyed.

They sat nestled between the roots of a tree for a moment of respite and began to fall asleep.

As Alice relaxed, the moment of her capture again flashed through her mind. She had been at the edge of the woods, holding her Bible. She had carried that Bible practically nonstop for over a year, until that fateful day. Her father and stepfather were both clergymen, so she had studied it all the time, memorizing things. At first she did it to please, but recently she was starting to find passages to counter Jed's more domineering view of humankind's role in nature. The more she read, the more she was able to formulate her own ideas and argue with him. She was just beginning to see that the Bible gave instructions to protect the earth and animals when she was taken.

"Alice! Bloody Knuckles is dead," Tom had announced, running over to her from the direction of the hot springs. He was breathing heavily and had his hands on his knees while he reported the awful news. "James somehow did it. Bloody Knuckles knew that James had taken his letter from G and went after him. Red is back here, but I don't know where James is. I'm worried he's hurt. I'm going to tell Mattie and Jed."

Tom was so sincere. She remembered how his dark black hair fell sloppily over his eyes. He had darted away before she could respond, so Alice had gone searching for James.

Suddenly, there they were, riding toward her, high

up on their horses: the Long Coat Gang. Slinger and Farley had spotted her as she came across a small slope. Red was with them on his horse. He was quiet. The men exchanged words, and circled around her, malice in their eyes. All she remembered after that were big, sweaty, hairy arms lifting her up. She tried to scream but they covered her mouth. Then there was darkness and horses clopping. *If only I could fly,* she had thought. Suddenly she found herself having the same wish in her current situation. *I know I have friends in this wilderness, I can feel it.* Alice drifted off to sleep between the tree roots. "I know they're out there," she said aloud.

"What?"

"What?"

"You're talking in your sleep, Alice," she thought she heard Tom say.

"Oh." She opened her eyes for a moment and thought she saw Tom leaning against a tree.

"Okay, Tom," she said and closed her eyes.

"I'm not Tom. I'm Red."

"Okay. Thanks for telling me everything. I'll go and look for James." She fell back into a slumber, gently resting on the folds of the roots between two trees.

~ *Chapter 8* ~

A JOURNEY BEGINS

The conversation with Hayden went perfectly, and within days, everything was set into motion. James left the letter for his mother and Jed, and walked out into the brisk air. On his way to meet up with his future traveling companions, James thought of all of the events that had led up to this moment: the trip across the country from New York, watching bison get shot wantonly from his train. He remembered how Alice had shuddered! He thought back to when his family arrived in Bozeman and met Tom. Now they were going together into the depths of Yellowstone, a park without a fence around it, a park that was larger than the states of Rhode Island and Delaware combined! It was what he had dreamed of doing since he first looked at the photographs and maps of the park in Miles' Bozeman newspaper shop. He felt guilty for this brief excitement about the expedition, knowing that the primary reason he was going was to find Alice. *If only she could be here,* James thought, *and we were going to the geysers together knowing she was alive and well.* He looked at his wristband and tried to send his thoughts her way.

Tom was waiting for James by the hot springs, where the men were set to gather for their journey. Mr.

Crissman, the photographer, rode over with two other fellows in tow. "Good afternoon, boys, and welcome. James, Tom, you'll be spending most of your time with these two gentlemen. Of course, you're welcome to help me photograph anytime, especially now that I don't have Elizabeth with me, as she's staying back with her mother," Crissman said in his sweet, quiet voice. "This is Chen. Best cook and laundryman around."

James looked over at a rugged Chinese boy with missing teeth, who had dismounted his horse. He must have been about seventeen. *I don't think he was on the important persons list,* James thought. At the mention of his name, Chen smiled and nodded his head at the boys. They nodded back.

"And you already know Patterson," Crissman said. James nodded at Patterson, who gave the boys a salute from atop his horse.

I feel so much safer knowing Patterson is here, James thought to himself, *a solider from Fort Ellis and a friend.* Patterson had been with James through the journey down from Bozeman and he always stood out for his fierceness and nobility. He was a tall, athletic man with upright posture and brown hair.

"Do you think Patterson knows that your parents

don't know?" Tom whispered. James shrugged, nervously. He was anxious to get further out of camp and away from the possibility of his mother seeing him.

Crissman's goatee moved up and down as he spoke. "You must have done something incredible to get on this trip. Dr. Hayden said there were many people interested in joining the expedition as assistants, so he must really have taken a liking to you, especially given your age." He gave the boys a little wink and leaned forward, looking elfish. "Good thing I was photographing at the hot springs and they needed a photographer. It looks like we all got lucky." He tipped his hat and rode away. Chen and Patterson remained behind to ready themselves for the trip.

James and Tom looked at each other and smiled. They tipped their hats to each other like the grown-ups did. *I couldn't have come without Tom,* James thought, realizing all that his friend was risking for this journey. But he also knew that this journey was everything Tom could have ever wished for. *Now I am actually going to see this land of curiosities,* James thought. *Now I am going to see why all of these government men have come out here, and why it was established as the world's first national park.*

After the final preparations, the party left the hot springs full of energy. It was the 29th of July, and the sun was warming their backs on the first leg of the journey. They rode for about five miles, just to get some of the traveling out of the way, and made camp on Black Tail Deer Creek near the Yellowstone River. James felt a chill as the sun began to set. James and Tom had no tents—just a mass of blankets and buffalo robes under the stars. This was how it would be for the rest of the trip. There were only four tents, and they were meant for the leaders of the expedition.

We're definitely not going to make it on the important people list, James mused. His nose was cold, as it was the only thing sticking out from his buffalo robes. James, Tom, and Chen all slept near each other for warmth. James wondered about his foreign companion. Chen didn't speak much English, which made it difficult for James to find out more about him. He wondered how Chen had made it on the expedition, and figured it was because he was an excellent packer and cook.

The first night was extremely cold. The water in their bucket completely froze and James couldn't help but think of Alice. *I hope she gets over her problem with wearing furs and that she's wearing a giant buffalo robe, wherever she is.* He fell asleep that night waiting to hear the trot of an approaching horse coming to take him back to Bozeman. He would be so embarrassed to have his mother and Jed come after him, but a large part of him missed their comfort. He was still only thirteen, and being out in the open wild made him feel his age.

His thoughts also drifted to Elizabeth Crissman and her soft curly hair. She had stayed back at Mammoth Hot Springs with her mother when her father left with the group. *What will she think when she finds out I went on a government expedition with her father?* James felt impressive for the risk he was taking. At one point, he heard the trees cracking in the wind and his ears perked up, still waiting to hear those horses. *What would she think if I was forced to come back?* Every snap of a branch or neigh of a horse made him open his eyes in anticipation. But no one ever came to collect James and Tom. Lying there in the cold mountain night, James had to admit he was a little disappointed that he wouldn't be saved from his own recklessness.

Chapter 9

MOUNTAIN LION

Alice and Red awoke from their rest to a terrifying shriek. They jumped up as the sun was setting and scrambled together in fear. They heard another shriek.

"Is that a person?" Alice whispered.

"I don't think so," Red answered.

"Come on." She grabbed Red by the arm as he slung his sack over his shoulder. "Up," she said. Quickly, without much time for thought or deliberation, they climbed their way up a tree. They huddled in between a few large branches as a large yellow beast came walking by.

"It's a mountain lion!" they whispered to each other at the same time. The lion pawed its way to where they had just been sitting and sniffed around, then let out its terrible shriek. *It sounds so much like a person,* Alice thought to herself. *But not a pleasant-sounding person.* It was like a tortured person, shrieking, distorted. They covered their ears.

"GET OUT OF HERE!" Red shouted at the beast.

"AHHblahblah!!" Alice made noises to frighten it away. The beast stalked them on one side and they quickly shifted their position. It let out a low rumbling growl.

"LEAVE, LION!"

"GET OUT!" They tore off branches and threw them down at the beast. Alice's heart was pounding like a drum. Her eyes were alert with fear. The lion roared back at them. It would be so easy for this mighty beast to eat them for supper.

"Let's try being quiet," Alice said. They clutched the branches, unmoving.

What fate, Alice contemplated. She remembered walking down the crowded streets of New York only a year or so earlier. *How strange that I will be eaten by a lion in the middle of the wilderness. Nature can be so frightening.* As a result of her experiences out West, Alice had a whole new sense of awe for the wild and what it truly was: wild. In its uncharted territory, she was just another animal, another beast. It was either eat or be eaten, frighten or be frightened. *I wish I knew how to speak its language,* she thought to herself.

The suspense was unbearable. The lion paced below, snarling.

"What are you doing?" Alice asked Red, who was reaching into the bag slung over his shoulder. Red took out his bottle of whiskey and took a large gulp. Alice couldn't stop herself from gasping. He put his fingers to his lips. Then he lit a match. As he spat out the alcohol from his mouth in a spray, he lit it on fire and it exploded.

"Wow!" Alice mustered. The lion must have thought the same thing as it darted away, shrieking. Red repeated the trick and the lion scampered off into the woods. He put the whiskey back in his bag and they huddled in the branches of the tree. Everything seemed very quiet and still. Their ears were open for any sounds of the lion's return. Finally, Alice looked over at Red.

"Think he's gone?"

"I think so." They were both clutching the tree with all their might. Alice finally loosened her grip a little and her hands were shaking. Her whole body was shaking, even her voice.

"You know so much about how to survive out here. There's so little I know," Alice said.

"Well, I've spent my whole life traveling and hunting with my pa."

"Did he teach you that trick?" Alice wondered with some awe.

Red looked at her sternly. "Never try that without me. It's very dangerous. I burned off my eyebrows the first time I tried it and almost went blind."

They heard another snap of a twig and were alert again, but it was just the noises of the forest.

"To answer your question, yes, I learned the trick from him. My pa and I survived a lot of odd situations. I sort of thought he could never die after everything that I had seen him get through."

"I'm sorry," Alice whispered, her voice still quivering.

"That's okay," Red said. "I hated his guts." Alice was quiet.

"Here, hold this." He handed her the whiskey bottle. He turned to the side and Alice saw a large cut down the side of his arm.

"Oh, wow!" she said, looking at his wound.

"I think I scraped it when we were climbing up. I can't really pour and hold on at the same time. Can you pour some of the whiskey on my arm? That way it won't get infected." Alice took some of the alcohol and used the side of her dress to pat it onto his arm. He winced in pain. She suddenly felt overwhelming compassion for him.

"I'm sorry," she said again. He didn't say anything back. *I want to learn how to survive in the wild,* she thought to herself. *I need to learn the language of the wild. If Red can do it, I know I can.* The night was falling upon them again, like a slow guillotine. They didn't have a fire, and they were both too terrified to leave the tree.

"Maybe we should alternate sleeping and try to keep watch," Alice said.

"Okay," Red said, putting everything away again.

"Oh no, it looks like you spilled the alcohol all over yourself!" Alice looked down and saw that Red's pants were all wet.

"No, I didn't."

"I'm sorry, I must have done it," she said.

"No, you didn't." He paused. "I . . . had an accident. I peed."

"Oh." Alice let this sink in for a moment. She realized that Red had wet his pants from fear. Despite her terribly chapped and painful lips, she couldn't help the corners of her mouth from turning up. Finally, she couldn't hold it back anymore. All of her nervousness had built up into one giant laugh. It burst out of her— a loud laugh that was swallowed by the vast wilderness and the night.

"It's not funny," Red said. His voice had that sharp, menacing tone from earlier.

Tears were coming to her eyes with laughter. But she couldn't stop herself. She was coughing and laughing and crying. Finally she calmed down. *Well, if I get eaten tonight, at least I died laughing!* she thought, and let out one final cough. Red was quiet. *What a crab,* she thought. *He needs to learn to laugh at himself.* But her elation was only temporary. It was soon replaced by feelings of guilt and hunger, followed by yet another sleepless night.

~ *Chapter 10* ~

MEAT

While journeying on their way down the south bank of the Yellowstone River, the group came upon a beautiful canyon. It was the third canyon that James had seen so far. There was a view of the winding river between the pine-covered mountains. With every breath of fresh air, James felt amazed that he was out experiencing the wonders of nature in such good and professional company.

Coming through the thicket by the Crevice Gulch, Tom spotted a herd of antelope grazing. He whispered to the other men and they readied their guns. Chen fired twice, but both of his shots missed.

"Agh!" he exclaimed in frustration.

Meanwhile, Patterson was concentrating on one particular antelope. He had his sights fixed on it and dismounted his horse to run off in hot pursuit.

"I hope he catches that, or it's sardines and bread for lunch," Tom said. James agreed. All was quiet as the sun beat down on James' head and made him dizzy. He was relieved at the sight of Patterson walking back with half of an antelope. The animal was too large to bring back in its entirety. It was a bit gruesome to see only part of the animal dangling over his shoulder, but they were hungry. Patterson's hunt had been successful, and it was a great reward to eat meat after the long day.

As James, Tom, Patterson, and Chen sat down to eat, two other members of the Hayden Expedition rode up to join them in their feast: a wealthy British landowner named William Blackmore, and an expert hunter and guide named Bill Hamilton.

"Most excellent catch," Blackmore noted hungrily as the two dismounted their horses and sauntered over.

Blackmore was a good friend of Dr. Hayden's. James felt intimidated by his British accent and well-groomed dark beard. He was clearly a man of politics and poise, even though his belly protruded like a pear from under his vest. He traveled a lot to Washington and New York, and fancied himself an expert on Indian affairs. But Blackmore was legitimately powerful; his success as a landowner helped to fund the expedition they were currently enjoying, so James sat up straight to prove that he was worthy of participating.

"I couldn't have done it better myself, Patterson," Hamilton the mountain man said. His face was sun-streaked and splotchy. He had a bump on his nose where it looked like it had been broken.

Everyone sat down for a meal amidst a sea of abandoned elk antlers, except for Chen, who kept his distance. Tom picked up an antler and tossed it.

"These seem to be everywhere over here," Tom commented. "Do you know the difference between horns and antlers?"

"No," James said.

"These fellas are antlers," Tom said picking one up. "They grow out of the animal's head like a part of their skull," he held it up to his head, demonstrating. "They're made of bone. They fall off and then grow back every year."

"Interesting," James said, always amazed with the facts that his friend retained. "That explains why there are so many about."

"Horns, on the other hand, are bone on the inside, but the outside is a casing that's like the material of your fingernails."

"Ew."

"Horns also don't usually fall off like antlers. They just keep growing, like fingernails. You know, buffalo horns, sheep horns …" James thought of the sheep that had called to him in his dream.

"Most interesting, Tom," Blackmore complimented.

"I have somethin' else interesting that I bet you've never tried before," Hamilton interrupted. "This here, my friends, is a delicacy."

The carcass of the antelope was splayed out over on the side, and Hamilton reached his hand into its slimy insides and pulled out the animal's liver. James' stomach turned.

Hamilton's hand was calloused with a layer of dirt from his many days in the outdoors. His fingernails were worn down to the skin. The blood from the liver oozed down his wrist and onto his muscular, hairy forearm. Despite the disgusting sight, James found he was mighty hungry and ready to eat just about anything.

"I do believe that you mountaineers have a fondness for rare meat," Blackmore said, chuckling.

"Most definitely," Patterson agreed.

Hamilton took a bestial bite of the piece of liver.

"You astonish me with rudiments of life. Every year, it's mining or prospecting in the summer, then hunting in the fall to sustain you through the winter, and then back at it again. And you are the most sober group of men I have ever encountered. It's delightful," Blackmore said.

"Why, thanks," Hamilton beamed. He took a knife out of the utility belt around his waist and sliced Blackmore a piece of the liver.

Blackmore sank his teeth into it and chewed as James and Tom looked on anxiously. "I must say, this is a most appetizing morsel," Blackmore commented.

Hamilton wiped his nose with the back of his forearm. "I done told you so!" The mountain man took another bite himself, and some of the juice dripped onto his grizzled beard. Hamilton's hair was stiff from being outside for so long, and his beard looked like a mass of tiny wires springing out from around his face. James noticed that his own hair took on a burnt quality from his days in the wind and sun. *I wonder if I'll look like him by the end of the trip,* James thought. *Only I don't have a whisker to speak of.*

Blackmore could see James looking at Hamilton admiringly. "You are looking at a master hunter and outdoors man," Blackmore said as he patted Hamilton on the shoulder. "Mr. Hamilton here is a relic from another era, when the old trappers ruled the West."

"Not bad for a little foster boy from Humansville, Missouri, huh!" Hamilton laughed to himself, and pieces of the antelope liver revealed themselves in his blackened teeth. *Bloody Knuckles was from Missouri,* James remembered, momentarily shuddering.

"Mr. Hamilton has killed at least 600 bears in his lifetime. I've seen his incredible sportsmanship on this trip," Blackmore said, impressed.

"I'm just doing what I can to compete with those Bottler brothers," Hamilton laughed. "The one Bottler just killed a she-bear and two cubs on this expedition. He's around here somewhere. . . . "

They do hunt a lot, James recalled. *Maybe too much.*

The Bottler brothers had a ranch between Bozeman and Mammoth Hot Springs. Some called it the last outpost of civilization before entering Yellowstone. James had met the brothers, Phillip and Frederick, on his original trip down from Bozeman, and everyone commented on the lavish meals they prepared. Frederick was joining them on the current expedition.

"Oh, quite right, quite right. I have missed the stories of your hunts since I last saw you, before I went to visit the Crow Indian Agency," Mr. Blackmore said. "I met with the tribal council to hear some of their worries." This made James perk up.

"And what did they complain about now?" Hamilton sneered accusingly. James immediately got a sense of how Hamilton felt about Indians.

"Well, the usual. But I have noticed that there are more and more complaints about the decrease of their primary food source: the buffalo. The Indians make use of the entire animal; much of their livelihood depends upon it. You may find this raw antelope liver unappetizing, James, but a buffalo can feed twelve persons without a fire. The nose, the liver, even the paunch. A truly incredible animal. It's a shame that it's disappearing. The buffalo range is now a third of what it was twelve years ago."

James again thought of Bloody Knuckles and he looked at Tom. Bloody Knuckles and the Long Coat Gang had been hired to kill the buffalo in order to get the Indians off the land. The boys didn't know who had hired the gang, but it appeared to be a mysterious character named G, based on a note that James had intercepted. Bloody Knuckles had tried to kill James for stealing his letters and uncovering the plan, but James had narrowly escaped this fate. Instead, it was Bloody Knuckles who met his demise.

It wasn't my fault, James reassured himself. *It was an accident.* James had cleverly startled the horse Bloody Knuckles was riding. As a result, the man was catapulted head-first into a boiling hot spring. James helplessly watched as his enemy's face peeled off and his eyes turned white. He had tried to save him, but it was no use.

James poked at his piece of liver tentatively. "I don't think I'm that hungry," he finally assessed, his vivid memories overtaking his appetite.

"Okay. I'm going to take your piece over to Chen," Patterson said, grabbing James' slimy piece of liver and hopping up toward Chen.

"Tom?" Patterson challenged. Tom closed his eyes and ate his piece of liver in one big gulp.

As the group finished lunch and continued down to Elk Creek, James and Tom veered off to talk.

"Did you hear what he said about the buffalo?" James asked Tom.

"So, it must be true. And look, it's working. If that's what the Crow Council told him, then the plan is succeeding and the Indians are going hungry."

"Tom, we still never found out who Bloody Knuckles was working for and who is behind this. We have to stop it."

"For the Indians or for the buffalo?" Tom asked.

"Both," James answered confidently. He thought of Alice and their pledge to protect the animals, nature, and people.

"Can you imagine if Alice heard that story about Hamilton killing 600 bears? I'm sure he didn't eat all of those bears either. It was just for sport." James winced.

"James, you're going to make a lot of enemies if you go after sportsmen. And I've seen you enjoy a hunt before. We are, in fact, just animals as well, aren't we? Charles Darwin proves it. Our instincts are to survive and attack and eat and beat our opponents. It's exciting and you can't take that out of human character," Tom explained. James was disturbed by his friend's perspective.

"Don't look so judgemental," Tom challenged. "It's best for the sportsmen to protect the animals, too. If they kill them all, there's no more game. Literally."

The group arrived at Elk Creek and joined up with the rest of the expedition. The area was a beautiful, grassy valley across from Sheep Mountain. James was again reminded of his dream in the tent. *What did that sheep mean in my dream, and why was it calling to me?* James wondered. *Who were those geyser men?*

Tom interrupted James' thoughts.

"Do you know why the mountains are that rusty color?" Tom asked.

"Why?" James was eager to get to the Tower Waterfalls.

"Because they are volcanic rocks with a lot of iron in them. When they get beat up by the weather, the iron turns them that color," Tom explained. "At least I think that's why. Try leaving something with iron in it outside for a while and you'll see what I mean."

The canyon was about a mile long, and it started at the mouth of Tower Creek, opposite Tower Falls. The walls jutted up straight toward the sky from the bottom of the water, and the river had a sparkling emerald green tint. Tower Falls was the first major sight in Yellowstone that James and Tom had recognized from reading the maps back in Miles' office all those months ago.

The waterfall plunged with a straight, clear drop. The boys stood for a moment and gazed at the force of nature falling between the rocks and trees.

"I'm slightly unimpressed," Tom confessed quietly to James.

"I've been to Niagara Falls," James replied. "This is . . . " And he shook his hand back and forth, indicating it was so-so in comparison. *Maybe I'm expecting too much,* James thought. *Maybe I'm expecting too much out of everyone and everything.*

~ *Chapter 11* ~
STALKED

In the morning, Alice and Red descended from their tree. They were stiff and hungry, so they ate some saved roots and drank water that Red had gathered in his canteen. They tiptoed nervously around where the mountain lion had been. Alice glanced at Red. He was covered in soot and dried urine, and his arm was gashed open. His eyes had dark circles under them, and he looked green. She could only imagine how haggard she appeared.

"We have to keep going until they find us," she urged.

"Right."

The two wearily picked themselves up and started

to walk. The grass crunched under them as they trod on in silence.

"What's that?" Alice murmured.

"What?" Red answered.

"I thought I heard something, Red," Alice said. They waited, ears perked, but all they saw was a rabbit as it darted off into some brush. They came out into a clearing and determined their best direction. *If only I had a compass,* Alice thought.

They walked on a bit and then Alice stopped again.

"I hear something," Alice whispered.

"You are just hungry and delirious, and, as I said once before, annoying."

She remembered how she had laughed at him the night before for peeing in his pants.

At least I don't smell like urine, she wanted to shout. But instead, she angrily stuck her tongue out at him. She hated his whole freckled face.

Then he stopped in his tracks.

"Alice, I think I see something," he said quietly. "Pretend like you don't notice and just keep on walking. I think the mountain lion is stalking us."

The word "stalking" alone made Alice's legs all

wobbly again. They walked a few more paces, and in an instant, Alice saw the huge beast pouncing to attack. She saw a flash of teeth and claws as an arrow sped just above her head and pierced the lion all the way through. The animal fell to the ground in a moaning thud. Alice felt conflicted. She hated that it was in pain, but then again, she was almost its breakfast! Another arrow came from behind the brush and the animal was still.

"Indians!" Red shouted. He quickly prepped his gun, even though there was no ammunition in it.

"Red, what are you doing? This is our chance to be saved. They can help us."

"I'm not going to be helped by any Indians."

Alice ignored Red and started signing the only word she knew in Indian sign language. With her palm facing forward, she slowly motioned downward, like she was petting an invisible animal. It was what a Bannock man signed to her back in Bozeman, when his tribe was going to hunt buffalo. It meant, "You have nothing to be afraid of, be calm."

Most of the Indians didn't come down, but held back, keeping higher ground. She heard the bark of a loud dog.

"Red, put the gun down, they just saved our lives. And I don't think you want one of those arrows going through you." They looked back and saw that the draw of the powerful bow had sent the arrow entirely through the large beast, from one side to the other. Red reluctantly pointed the gun down, mostly from exhaustion, but wouldn't let go of it. He tried to be brave.

"Alice, stand behind me," he said.

But Alice wasn't sure what to do next, so she got on her knees and bowed.

"Red, come on."

"I'm not bowing to any Indians," he said. He just stood there. Eventually, some of the hunters came forward to see their kill. One of them spoke a little English.

"You. Come," he said.

"Lost!" Alice said. "Alone." She tried to gesture being alone and looking around for the right way to go. The Indians were amused by her antics, which eased some of the tension. Two of them even laughed.

"They must have been tracking us for a while and known we were alone anyway," Red said, feeling a bit foolish. There were three men, each with a dog, and they guided Alice and Red back to where they were camped. The men wore leggings, and their long, dark hair flowed wildly around their faces. One had a feather hanging in his hair. Another wore an old U.S. Army jacket from the Civil War, which stood out in contrast to the traditional Indian garb. And a third man wore a Western-type button-up shirt.

Alice was surprised by the Indians around her, but she remained calm. She felt she could trust them. She turned to Red and smiled broadly.

"We're going to be okay," she said.

Red wiped the smile from her face with his quick response, "I don't think so. We don't know what these Indians want from us. They may just take our matches and flour and our knife and leave us in the cold—or worse."

Maybe Red was right. Around the campfire at Mammoth Hot Springs, she had heard some horrible stories about Indian raids. She remembered a particularly horrible one about miners whose heads ended up on the points of sticks. Alice was fond of her head and didn't really want it detached from her body. Mostly, though, she had just heard about Indians stealing horses. *I didn't realize there were still Indians living here in the park,* she thought.

The hunters spoke for a minute amongst themselves, then motioned for Alice and Red to follow them.

Chapter 12

THE MINING CAMP

After Tower Falls, the expedition arrived at Camp Number Nine: Meadow Creek. From there, James, Tom, Chen, and Patterson followed a small group led by Dr. Hayden to the mining camp at Clark's Fork. Mines always scared James a little because they were dangerous, and unpredictable men were always around, but Tom was curious about the minerals and insisted they follow. So far, not even a sign of Alice had appeared. *At this point, one way is as good as another,* James thought. He remembered his dream on the last night at Mammoth Hot Springs and how the needle of his compass had spun around in circles with no direction. *We have no direction,* James thought. He was beginning to feel discouraged about the whole adventure.

On the way to the mines, they tried their luck at fishing, and Tom caught six fish in an hour. James caught five. The other men did just as well and the fish averaged about a pound each, so everyone felt sated and uplifted in spirits. They continued riding along, telling stories and collecting insect specimens in jars.

When they stopped for a moment to stretch, Chen saw a piece of cloth hanging from a tree branch. He reached over and plucked it off the branch to examine it further. It was a bluish color. He thought the cloth had a nice pattern, but it was very worn. He shrugged and tossed the cloth to the ground and watched as it fluttered away in the wind.

They were only a few miles away from the mines when a man named Jack Baronett came to greet Dr. Hayden. He was a fiery man with a Scottish accent, and he kept a ranch nearby. He gave Dr. Hayden a few more specimens to take back as relics from the campsite, to prove the worth of the mining camp to the government.

"The valley of the lower Yellowstone will probably soon be traversed by a railroad, more especially if the mineral deposits in this district realize in richness and extend beyond the expectations of the miners at present," Mr. Blackmore commented.

"Well, Mr. Blackmore, we're sure trying," Baronett answered. James was reminded of his old friend Aldous Kruthers, who worked for the Northern Pacific Railway. Like most men, Kruthers believed that the railroad was the hope for tourism and progress. This excited James greatly.

There were about thirty men working at the Clark's Fork Mining Camp, which was not a large crew. There were a handful of mines set up, mostly for copper. Mr. Baronett gave them a tour, explaining that they were lode mines. Unlike placer mining, where individuals could sift through loose surface soil or gravel, lode mining required many miners working together to extract precious metals from tunnels in the earth.

As James walked by listening to the tour, a few of the miners waved. He thought a few of the men looked familiar, but it was hard to tell. They were covered in sweat and dirt. The mines were dark. There was a metallic taste to the air.

"James, look, it's some of the prospectors from Mammoth who disappeared after Bloody Knuckles died," Tom said quietly to James.

"And when Alice disappeared," James confirmed. "I'm glad you noticed. I thought they looked familiar."

"We should ask if they know anything about Alice," Tom suggested. James thought this was a fantastic idea.

"Pardon me, Mr. Baronett." James interrupted the tour. "Tom and I are going to explore on our own for a while."

As soon as James and Tom broke away from the group, one of the prospectors took notice of them.

"Hey! I know you! I remember you and your sister." He walked over to James to shake his hand. "I'm George McClarey. Good to see you again." He stepped forward to shake James' hand, then realized he was covered in grime.

"Sorry," he apologized, wiping his palm on his trousers. He was a very ruddy, round man. His cheeks were burnt by the sun and his yellow hair revealed every speck of dirt. He looked to James like a pink elephant, if such a thing existed. James was renewed with a sense of optimism at the man's kindness.

"We thought we recognized you from back at Mammoth, too!" James said excitedly.

"Phew, another day just trying to make a dollar," the man said, wiping his brow with a handkerchief from his pocket. "But we're pretty excited about hitting silver. Well, what brings you all the way out here? Where are your folks?"

James tried to avoid the questions.

"Well, it's a long story. But, I'm wondering if you can help me. The day that you left Mammoth Hot Springs, my sister Alice actually went missing. I don't know if you remember Bloody Knuckles, but his gang also went missing on that same day. Do you know anything that might help us?" James was putting on his best reporter face.

"Oh, well," George started, "I know they were some real bad men, that gang. We stayed around them sometimes because they were good hunters and we needed some extra people in camp, but we tried to keep our distance."

"Us too," Tom said.

"And that Bloody Knuckles fella ... I heard what happened to him." He gave James a big grin and wink. James should have felt flattered but he just felt guilty. *It was an accident. I didn't mean to kill him,* he repeated to himself. Sometimes in his nightmares, James would still hear the sounds of Bloody Knuckles' dying shrieks. His memory was seared with the image of the man thrashing and boiling alive. It was terrible.

"So why did you leave on the same day as the gang?" Tom inquired, picking up the lead, as James was distracted by his own thoughts.

"Well, once we heard that Knuckles was dead, we didn't want to stick around to find out what would happen. It seemed like a good idea to get out of there, so we went on our way. Didn't see where the Long Coat Gang went." James and Tom looked a little disappointed.

"Real sorry to hear that your sister went missing," George added. But James wasn't ready to give up. *If we find the gang, they may have some answers about Alice,* James reasoned. *Even if they are despicable characters, they might know something.*

"So you had no idea where the gang was headed?" James said.

"They did talk about this place called the Hole in the Wall out in Dakota. Actually now that I think about it, that real scraggly guy with the whiny voice mentioned a place once: Grizzly Ranch. I remember the name because he brought it up one day and then Bloody Knuckles threw a bottle at his head. Knuckles said he was never to say that name again out loud. So I remembered that. Grizzly Ranch."

"George!" Another prospector called from inside the mine. "I need a hand with this!"

"Boys, best of luck. I've got to get back to work. It was great to see you. Give my regards to your father, that preacher. Real nice fella. You're mighty lucky to have him as your pa." James cringed. *You didn't know my real father,* James thought.

"Thanks for your help," Tom said.

"Not a lick of a problem. I hope you find your sister."

George wiped his palms on his pants again, shook both of their hands, and lumbered elephant-like back to his place in the mine.

The side trip to the mines had been a great adventure and had encouraged James. He thought about the conversation he'd had with George all the way back to Cascade Creek near the Yellowstone Falls. There, James' crew and Dr. Hayden's small party rejoined with Crissman, the photographer, and made camp. The stars were bright that night and James ruminated on this new bit of information about Grizzly Ranch.

James could see the outline of the whole Milky Way Galaxy as he lay in his cozy, yet uneven, bed. *I can't believe it's the end of the summer. I have to find Alice soon before the days get shorter,* James thought. *Grizzly Ranch, Grizzly Ranch.* James turned the words over and over in his head. He reached over to his satchel and pulled out his compass. He closed his eyes.

"Show me where Alice went," James said aloud to the compass. He opened his eyes and looked down. The compass just faithfully pointed north, toward the bright little star in the sky. James sighed.

"Nice try," Tom said, rolling over and rustling his blankets.

"I thought you were sleeping," James said.

"Never too tired to make you feel stupid!" Tom quipped. The late summer insects were chirping all around them.

"Hey, thanks for coming out here with me," James said. "I know your family is probably nervous back in Bozeman, and we're probably the youngest people who've ever been out here before. There's people in our party that are making maps as we go along, so this isn't exactly safe or predictable. At least we're getting to see more of the park, I guess." James twirled his wristband under his blanket. "I don't know what I would have done without you," he whispered.

"Don't get sappy on me, dung face," Tom said, turning his back to James.

James let out a little laugh. He rolled over to go to sleep and saw Chen a few feet away, his arm under his head, looking up at the stars. *I wonder if he feels lost in this wilderness, speaking a foreign language, away from the country where he grew up,* James thought. *At least I have Tom.* He fell into a deep slumber, still clutching the compass in his hand.

Chapter 13

THE SHEEPEATERS

Alice and Red walked on in silence, trailing behind the three Indian men who had saved them from that ferocious mountain lion. The men's long, dark hair swayed back and forth with their strides. Red clutched his gun nervously by his side. Despite Red's warnings about Indians, Alice didn't feel as scared anymore.

Two wolf-like dogs carried a long sled behind them. The mountain lion was splayed out, dead, on the sled, being dragged back to camp for food—an unconventional meal. Alice cringed watching its limp paws scrape against the dirt. Then she looked at its claws and remembered with terror how it had leapt toward her in attack.

When they arrived at the main Indian camp, Alice counted four women and seven children waiting for the men to return from the hunt. All were dressed in well-cut, tan-colored deer and sheep skins. A puff of steam rose from a stone bowl on a hot fire, transporting the smell of herbs and berries to Alice. Her stomach growled with hunger.

Alice looked around and saw a few wickiups strewn about. These were cone-shaped homes, built by long log poles all leaning up against each other. The logs were thin and brown with little knobs and rough bark. Alice had seen teepees from a distance when traveling across the country, but these looked a little different. They were covered with brushwood and grass, rather than cloth.

There were about twenty-five more wolf-like dogs dutifully scurrying about camp. Some of the enormous dogs were transporting items on their backs. There were no leashes; they were like a part of the clan. *True worker dogs,* Alice thought, as she watched a pair carry sticks over to their owners. Alice was absolutely delighted to be among friendly animals again. She smiled a little and looked at a couple of fuzzy puppies playing happily, jumping up and biting each other on the ears. One of the small pups approached Alice and sniffed her tattered boots. He was fluffy, with grey fur and white patches around his eyes like a raccoon.

"Hello," Alice said instinctually and bent down to pet the dog. But the Indians shooed the dog away and quickly then spoke amongst themselves. Alice and Red stood side by side awkwardly.

Exhausted and starving, Alice let out a wheezy cough. The women looked at each other nervously. A debate erupted among them.

"I think they're afraid we're sick," Red said.

"Well, I am," Alice replied, trying to muffle her cough.

"No, I mean, really sick. Try not to cough again."

"Okay," Alice said. The more she thought about not coughing, the more she wanted to cough. Part of her was happy that Red didn't really even think of her as that sick, though. *Maybe I'm actually getting better,* she wondered.

"Where are their horses?" Alice asked.

"I don't think they use horses," Red answered.

That makes sense, Alice thought. *Dogs are probably more useful in the mountains than horses.* She watched them pad about swiftly among jagged rocks and inclines.

A few of the women who had been grinding berries eyed Red and looked down at the weapon by his side. Although their stony expressions did not reveal how they felt, Alice could sense their apprehension.

"Red, maybe you should put down the gun."

He didn't answer, but he had that icy cold look in his eyes. Alice was afraid, but not as scared as she had been alone with Red in the wilderness, and definitely not as scared as she had been with the Long Coat Gang.

Two women, who appeared to be a mother and daughter, stepped forward from the delicious-smelling stone pots to join the men who had returned from hunting. Their hair was just as dark as the men's, parted in the middle and flowing downward, like leaves gently falling from a tree. They wore large quill necklaces.

Red and Alice were directed to stand and wait as the families met and discussed the new arrivals. *What can I do to show them we are peaceful?* Alice wondered. She had an idea and grasped the side of Red's bag. He quickly pulled away and shot her a nasty look. She pursed her lips together and he reluctantly let her rummage through his things. She took out the remaining roots and some of the sugar that Red had taken from their earlier provisions. She placed the goods a few feet in front of where she and Red stood, as a gift to the tribe. The group watched her movements, and stopped talking. The woman and her daughter stepped forward.

"Hello," the daughter said. Alice was so relieved. *The girl spoke English!* "Thank you for goods," she continued. "You are alone. You will live with us." She said it as a command, not as a question. Alice nodded enthusiastically, feeling Red's muscles tighten next to her.

"Yes! Yes, please!"

"Come and share our food," she said. The girl was around Alice's age. She had an oval face and dark skin, and her eyes were a pale green. They all looked over at Red, who did not move.

"You will join our family," the girl said. One of the men stepped forward to take Red's gun, but he clutched it to his chest. Red looked horrified.

"I am Alice," she said pointing to herself. "This is Red."

The girl, her mother, and the men did not immediately introduce themselves. Once she saw that Alice was waiting for a response, the girl named everyone in the clan. "I am Green Blossom," she said. "My father was a white man, but he is with the spirits now. He taught me English. Mother and sister know to speak, too, but not like me. Mother is named Standing Rock. Sister is named Smiles Like Chipmunk." Alice could see easily why this was the older sister's name. "This is my new father, Runs With Arrow, this is my uncle, Spotted Eagle, and this is my cousin, Bear Heart." Bear Heart had high cheekbones and looked very unhappy. These were the three men who had found Alice and Red. Green Blossom continued naming the rest of the women and children. Alice was amazed at how welcoming the small group was.

"Can you take us back to my family? They are at Mammoth Hot Springs." Alice realized that they probably didn't know the name "Mammoth Hot Springs." Alice imagined the cascading terraces and McCartney and Horr's bathhouses. Her heart ached to go back. She briefly tried to describe the area, but Green Blossom stopped her.

"We cannot go to white people. My family is hiding. We did not want to be on reservation—the special place for Indians. We follow the sheep. The mountains are our home. If we go to white men, they will take us to reservation."

Alice's heart sank. She thought of her mother and James.

"You will be my sister," the girl announced. *I've never had a sister,* Alice thought, a little excited by the prospect. She and Red exchanged a brief glance. They both realized that they didn't have a choice. No matter how much they wanted to leave, they couldn't survive on their own; they needed provisions. Alice looked back at Green Blossom.

"Thank you," she said. *We'll stay with them for as*

long as we need ... until there is a chance to go home, Alice thought.

Later that night, Alice tried to use makeshift sign language to communicate with the Indians, but was mostly unsuccessful. She did learn that they had joined the Sheepeater tribe, Tukudika. Like the Buffalo Eaters and Salmon Eaters, the Sheepeaters were a division of the Shoshone tribe. True to their name, they stuck to the high mountains and fed on the bighorn.

Red remained taciturn, sitting alone, holding his gun close. After a while, the clan seemed to decide that he was harmless. They each came up to him and just stared at his freckled face. Red looked especially uncomfortable when the tribe members came and started to play with his red hair, fascinated. It made Alice want to laugh out loud, but she remembered how sour he got the last time she laughed at him. *Maybe he's had too many people in his life who have laughed at him,* she thought.

That night, Alice huddled in the wickiup with her new family. She felt protected and safe for the first time in days. The dogs outside were like armor against all the beasts in the wild. No mountain lions. As she reflected on the day, she realized that even though she wasn't sure of what to do, all of her actions had led them to this place of comfort. *I must have done something right,* she thought, feeling a renewed sense of confidence. *And Red was even following my lead!* She said her prayers and inhaled the woody scent of the walls. Finally, she slept.

~ *Chapter 14* ~

GRAND CANYON

James woke up in the morning at Cascade Creek, still turning the words over in his mind: *Grizzly Ranch, Grizzly Ranch.* Chen prepared a breakfast of bacon and beans, as they were entirely out of fresh meat. James' stomach grumbled even after eating. It was still dark out, but there was a hint of dawn on the horizon.

After breakfast, Tom tried to distract his friend from the lack of news about Alice by bringing him to see an incredible wonder. They went to see what Crissman had been taking photos of during their side excursion to the mines: the Yellowstone Falls. The Upper and Lower Falls were everything that James expected and more. A misty spray flew in his face. A booming sound echoed in his ears as the waters crashed down, churning and foaming at the bottom. Their beauty and force fueled his renewed sense of optimism that Alice was alive.

While the men set off photographing and taking notes, James and Tom went with Dr. Peale, the mineralogist, to explore the falls. Peale was very excited by the idea of the Grand Canyon of the Yellowstone.

"This gives an excellent opportunity to study the various rocks that underlie the valley," he said as he trotted along. Dr. Peale was remarkably young for someone with so much knowledge.

"If that's what a smarty looks like, then I want to be one," Tom said. James laughed. They took a dangerous path down to the top of the Lower Falls, to get the scope of what it looked like from above.

After scaling the side of the mountain's sharp edges through the trees, they approached the brink and looked over into the abyss. "It is here that we realize how small man is when in the presence of nature's grand master-pieces. Down, down goes the whirling mass, battling and writhing as the water dashes against the rocks with a noise like the discharge of artillery," Peale said solemnly.

"Hear, hear," Tom said, echoing Peale's sentiments.

At that moment, James understood why geology

was so powerful, and why Tom loved it. Geology, the study of rocks, put humankind in its place over time. It showed that human beings were but a blip—albeit a brilliant blip—in the great workings of the world around them. These rocks had been there many years before his birth—or even before human existence— and they would remain well after his death. James felt humbled. He realized that his story and Alice's story fit into the great epic of humankind's struggle for survival and significance.

"Thank you, evolution, for giving me a really great brain so I can appreciate this," Tom stated, with an ever-practical appreciation for grandeur.

"It's not that great of a brain," James teased.

After collecting geological specimens in the canyon, Dr. Peale, James, and Tom returned to find the food situation much improved. Bottler had killed five elk so they would finally get to fill their stomachs.

"It looks like a meat market," Tom observed.

"Indeed it does," Crissman said in his soft-spoken manner. His artistic eye flashed with delight. "It would make an excellent photograph. Bottler, sit in the middle of the elk here." Bottler followed the instructions and sat in the middle of his kill as James and Tom looked on.

"The successful hunter," Crissman declared as he snapped the shot. He took another two shots and several stereo views to make sure the moment had been captured.

Something about the whole scene made James uncomfortable. He thought of Alice and their pledges. He didn't like that death made a pretty and interesting picture. *It's a fine line between a successful hunt and slaughter,* James thought. *And another fine line between hunger and madness.* He looked at all the dead beasts and felt the saliva thickening in his mouth.

After they ate and their stomachs were filled, James and Tom left with a smaller group to explore the mud geysers, located at Camp Thirteen near the Yellowstone River. *I hope we're not traveling away from her,* James thought anxiously. In fact, he was heading right in Alice's direction.

Chapter 15

STAR EYE

Alice quickly adapted to life with the Sheepeater tribe. She and Red were immediately assigned daily chores as they made their traverse across the rugged mountains and red valleys. There was always work to do, which distracted Alice from how much she missed her family. Red reluctantly helped the men with hunting and fishing. Alice helped the women dig for roots and find berries and seeds. While bent over, grinding seeds, she constantly tried to come up with ways to get home. One positive thing was that Alice's new diet consisted of mostly vegetables, berries, and roots. She could avoid meat almost entirely. The tribe noticed this and started to call her "Root Digger."

Roots were particularly important at this time of year because the clan was making its way to a different location and needed transportable foods. The group was moving farther south in the Absaroka Mountain Range near Yellowstone Lake, to the mountain slopes covered with pine trees where they would be able to collect pine nuts.

On the third day with the tribe, Green Blossom approached Alice, and two pups followed her. One was the patch-eyed dog that had come over and sniffed Alice's boots when she first arrived.

"He went to you," Green Blossom said. "He is your working partner." Alice couldn't believe it. The best gift she had ever received was a rabbit, and now she was being given a puppy all for herself. There were often dogs around Mammoth that accompanied the other tourists or the army men, and she had looked at them covetously. She would play with them and lie on their stomachs when it was cold.

"What do you mean by a working partner?" Alice asked.

"She is not a friend. She is a hunter. She will obey your call. She will carry your belongings. She must be fed, every meal, before you. This is like . . . partner. You take care one another."

"I understand," Alice said.

"Go," Green Blossom said to the dog. Alice bent down and petted the beautiful puppy. She was so happy she almost jumped. She took a moment and spoke to the dog quietly.

"What should your name be? Hmmm? What should we call you? I'll call you ... Star Eye." The dog yelped in excitement.

"You are good at naming," Green Blossom's sister, Smiles Like Chipmunk, said. "You are not like your brother. You can talk to the animals like friends."

Alice looked startled. *My brother?* she thought. An image of James flashed through her mind. *She must be talking about Red,* Alice realized. Alice noticed that among the clan, family titles were interchangeable. A cousin was called a sister, an uncle a brother, and so forth. It was the Shoshone way. Alice found this inclusive and welcoming, but a bit confusing.

"This is special gift. To name," Green Blossom said. Alice thought about this for a minute and then remembered how she had helped name James' horse. "We do not name things how you do. My father showed me how white people name things."

"Yes, I think that people like to give a new name to

something because it makes them feel like they own it—like they've given it a new identity," Alice said. "It also makes things clear. If it's a place, everyone can look at it on a map and know where it is and they won't be lost," Alice said.

"Yes," Green Blossom replied. "Soon, I do not think that any of our old names will be here anymore." She stated this calmly.

"That's not true. There are a lot of Indian names for mountains and valleys and things," Alice replied.

"Maybe. But only shadows. Not directions."

I wish that I could be more like Green Blossom, Alice thought. Green Blossom was very well-respected in her clan. Since Alice and Red's arrival, she had become especially valued for her English. She had a special glow about her, something that was relaxed, but also strong and confident. *I don't think her legs would ever shake from fear,* Alice thought, remembering the night that she and Red were trapped in the tree. *I know I can learn from her.*

Chapter 16

"IT WENT THAT WAY"

The Hayden party spent three days at the mud geysers waiting for a supply train from Fort Ellis. James was frustrated because he wanted to keep searching for Alice, but they couldn't do much without provisions. He was also eager for any letters or news from his family, and whoever brought the goods down from Fort Ellis would also transport the mail.

The party was starting to look a bit dilapidated. Wakefield, the meteorologist, had a bandaged leg and his trousers were torn away. Dr. Hayden was covered with mud spots and a torn coat. Tom's shirt was gashed from when his horse had bucked him off a few days ago. Even Patterson, who was always so proud-looking and militarily well-dressed, was frayed around the edges. Chen had a cut on his hand from a fishing accident. And the worst of it: They were out of sugar. Luckily, the mud volcanoes were an entrancing distraction.

The mud volcanoes were bubbling masses of goop that made James think of his stepfather Jed's descriptions of hell. *He would have loved the geyser named Devil's Cauldron,* James contemplated. *I wonder what he's preaching about these days.* James' thoughts of Jed turned to worried thoughts about his mother. He wondered if she was healthy, if the baby she was carrying was okay, and if they'd had a safe journey back to Bozeman. He began to write a letter to his mother and Jed, hoping to send it off when the provisions arrived.

While they were waiting anxiously for mail and supplies, James went for a walk by himself, and saw Dr. Peale taking measurements of the mud geysers with the assistance of Mr. A. E. Brown, who worked as assistant topographer. Brown was always willing to share the maps they were creating with James and Tom. It reminded James of the old days when he and Tom sat in Miles' office back in Bozeman and dreamed of going to Yellowstone. He couldn't believe all that had happened since then.

As James stepped over some fallen timber, he heard the sound of trees rustling to his right.

"Tom, I know that's you. You can't fool me again," James said into the wild. But there was no answer.

"Tom?" James heard more scurrying in the bushes. He had left all of his supplies back at camp. *Should I get closer or back away?* he anxiously thought.

"Tom, if that's you..."

Out of the brush, James saw saw a black bear dart through the trees. He stood frozen in his footsteps. *I think I scared him,* James hoped. His heart was pounding against his rib cage. When it looked like the beast had passed, James quickly returned to camp, jumping at every little rustle he heard.

"Bear! Bear!" he announced, running back toward Peale and the rest. Everyone became excited by the news. Those who weren't collecting scientific data and specimens quickly loaded their guns and went out to find it.

"Where was it, boy?" one of the men asked, loading his gun. James was overcome with a sense of defiance. He was excited about the bear, too, and he wanted to see it up close. He was even excited by the idea of going out and hunting it for fun, but part of him wanted it to live. He thought of Alice. He thought of his pledge to protect the park.

"It went that way," James pointed, leading them in the opposite direction.

He looked at Tom, whose dark hair had grown so it was falling almost to the end of his nose, and the two of them had a moment of recognition. Tom held up his hand with the wristband and cocked his head to the side. James responded with the same gesture, confirming Tom's suspicion. What they didn't notice as they exchanged glances was that Chen was sitting on a fallen log nearby. He watched the exchange very closely. When the men returned empty-handed, Chen wondered what those wristbands were all about.

Chapter 17

RED BREAKS

The women were finishing up their daily tasks and preparing for the men to return from a hunt. Green Blossom's younger cousins were rolling around on a small blanket, their laughter filling the crisp air. Alice used buckskin strings to play cat's cradle with Green Blossom and Smiles like Chipmunk. They wove their fingers in between the strings, creating animal shapes and complicated patterns. Star Eye, Alice's new dog, snuggled up next to her and playfully nipped at her fingers during this brief moment of recreation.

Alice was feeling completely at ease, when the laughter was interrupted by sounds of the dogs greeting each other, and the hunters returning to camp. Star

Eye's ears perked up. Alice saw Red with the hunters, a deep scowl across his face. *Always a scowl on his face,* Alice thought, annoyed. There was a loud ruckus, and Alice realized it was Red who was causing it. The girls dropped the string game and came out to see what was happening. Star Eye bounded along dutifully. Everyone else in camp came out to investigate, as well.

"This is mad!" Red was shouting at the top of his lungs. He was waving around a bow in his hand and arrows were slung around his back. "I hate all you stupid Indians! I'm getting out of here, forget this! You hear me?" Alice joined the circle of people accumulating around Red. He saw her approach and glared at her with explosive intensity. "FORGET YOU TOO," he pointed at her and shouted. She jumped back, stunned. It was the first thing he had said to her since the day of their arrival with the Sheepeaters.

"Where is my gun? I'll aim it at your heads," he continued rabidly. Alice was horrified. She wished that she had no association with him at all.

"And why did you give me this . . . this piece of junk? This pointless wooden bow that can only kill little rodents? I want the bow that killed the mountain lion!

I want the bow made of horn! I want to shoot my gun. This pathetic thing is impossible!" He pounded the bow into the dirt, smashed it on a rock and stepped on the shattered weapon repeatedly. He yelled at it, broken on the ground.

"TAKE THAT, YOU WORTHLESS NOTHING!" he screamed at the bow, his face contorted. He stomped on it some more, jumping on it with both feet at the same time for added effect. *I think he's finally snapped. He's lost his mind,* Alice thought, nervous about what he might do next. Everyone had gathered around him. He started to pant angrily. There was a pause and then, without any warning, Red let out a scream. Star Eye barked at him with all his might, and Alice tried to hush her protective pup. After Red's guttural cry, he turned and stormed out of camp without looking back.

Everyone was shocked for a moment, watching the boy walk away into the foothills alone. "Bow breaker," Bear Heart said scornfully under his breath in Shoshone. Green Blossom instinctively translated for Alice, but Standing Rock, Green Blossom's mother, silenced her and the rest of the murmurs from the crowd. She stepped forward. "We will continue as we were," she said strongly. Standing Rock looked carefully at Bear Heart. After a last glance over the horizon, people disbanded and went about their business.

As we were? Alice thought. *But what about Red? What if he just leaves? Why does he have to be so difficult and mean?* She truly didn't understand him. He had been so cold to her since they arrived in camp. For days, she had tried to speak to him but he ignored her. His screams of rejection echoed in her heart, hurtfully. *I can't believe I have to pretend he's my brother,* she thought. *What a sorry replacement.* No one from the family implied that she was responsible for Red's behavior, but she felt as though she were. *Fine. Go off into the woods to die. See what I care. You don't just break bows, you break spirits. I have Star Eye, I have my new family. I don't need you anymore.* Alice watched Red walk away until he became a dot in the distance.

"Whose turn is it?" Alice said, calmly. Green Blossom looked at Alice and studied her for a moment. They went back to playing their game.

~ *Chapter 18* ~

"LONG LIVE BLOODY KNUCKLES!"

The Hayden Expedition finally received correspondence and extra goods from Fort Ellis. All were relieved to see the replenishment of sugar and basic necessities, but everyone was most delighted to get mail. James stood on the tips of his toes as they called out the names of each letter recipient.

"Thomas Blakely," the courier called out.

Tom took the letter with haste.

"Feels thick. Must be from Mother. I'll be able to tell you every detail of Bozeman gossip in just a few minutes, just wait," Tom said, rolling his eyes. "See you."

Despite his mocking, Tom tore open the letter and

rapidly started to read while he walked away to sit by a hot spring in solitude.

"James Clifton," the courier said. James snatched up his letters from the courier's hands. He had received three. He rushed away from the group to have some privacy as well.

He opened the first one and saw it was from his wily newspaper friend, Miles.

Dear James,

Well, aren't you just a renegade. We've heard about your adventures with the government folk out there, and we're mighty proud to have you representing our fine town of Bozeman among that lot. I trust that you and Mr. Tom Blakely haven't been eaten by bears yet, and if you were, then you probably won't be reading this and your mama will never forgive herself.

Bozeman is doing just fine without you, but will probably be better when you return. School is about starting, and Miss Elizabeth Crissman and her mother returned with your parents. I saw them just a few minutes ago and said I was fashioning you a letter. Miss Elizabeth said you were a real gentleman. I bet you were.

I'm looking forward to seeing some accounts of your adventures in writing, which is the only reason why I still care about your sorry soul. Although I do have a list here that tells me a few of your friends are the newspaper correspondents for some fancier papers than the grand Bozeman Avant Courier. Let's see. I have that Mr. Savage is writing for the Denver Rocky Mountain News, Mr. Beveridge is writing for a Kansas paper, a Mr. Adams is writing for the New York papers and the Philadelphia Inquirer. So you've got some competition. Don't let me down. Tell Alice I say howdy when you find her and tell Tom he's a weasel and always will be.

Your loyal friend,

Miles

James chuckled at his friend. Miles was such a character. It felt so good to read news from home. He couldn't help but let a smile spread across his face at the idea of Elizabeth talking to Miles about him. *She said I was a gentleman!* he thought gallantly.

James recognized the handwriting on the second letter immediately. He stared at it for a moment, letting it sink in. It was from his mother, Mattie. His heart pumped as he held it in his hand. A flash of fear pulsed through his mind. *Will she be angry with me?* He peeled it open tentatively.

Dearest James,

I hope this letter finds you in good heath and good spirits. Are you eating well enough? Be sure to wash regularly. You may be in the wilderness, but try to remain civilized.

It has been hot here in the days and I am restricted to much bed rest. The homestead is good and I have been furnishing as much as energy allows. But do not fear for me. The doctor called on me yesterday in the forenoon; he declared me in good health and said the baby is coming along fine.

James, you must forgive me. I think if I were in my right mind and body, I would have hurried after to retrieve you when you departed Mammoth Hot Springs. Please know that I wanted to with my very essence, but somehow I convinced myself that you were using sound judgment. Although I was gravely upset when I received your note, I realized I could not be too cross, for I would have done the same were it not for my condition. You are a brave boy; your father must be smiling down on you from heaven.

Jed and I pray for you and Alice in church every Sunday. I cannot tell you how many times I have dreamed that I would be at home cooking, reading, or sewing, and you and Alice would walk in the front door together. Knowing that you are searching constantly renews my sense of hope.

Please send our regards to Tom and thank him and all of those in your company for ensuring your safe and speedy return.

With never-ending love and affection,

Your Mother

James felt as if a bird that had been caged in his heart was suddenly let free. His worry for his mother's approval had been fluttering inside him incessantly. *I am giving her hope,* he thought. This, in itself, renewed his own sense of hope and his fierce determination. He was also tremendously relieved that she was feeling better. He stuffed the letter in his pocket for safekeeping and promised to read it whenever he felt lost. *It's amazing how a person can orient me just as much as a place or a compass,* he thought to himself, feeling grounded in this news from home.

James was so happy about hearing from his mother that he almost forgot about the third letter. It was also sent from Bozeman, but there was no signature. *That's curious,* James thought. The letter crumpled and tossed in the wind as he opened it. He gasped. All it said was four words, but it made his heart jump from inside his ribs.

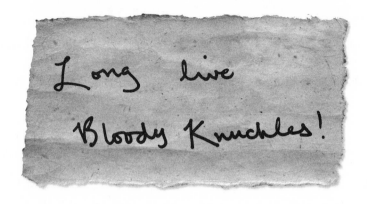

Was this a joke? James considered. *Maybe from Miles? No, even he wouldn't find that funny.* James' great sense of relief and comfort from only moments before vanished instantly.

His mind raced to think of who knew of his current whereabouts. *It couldn't have been one of the men on the trip. ... Why would they have sent it from Bozeman?*

He found Tom by the hot spring still reading Henrietta's long letter. He handed the hostile note to him nervously.

"Look, James, I'm sure it's just some friends of Bloody Knuckles or upset folks back in Bozeman who have nothing better to do with their time," he consoled. But the boys looked at each other with apprehension. Someone was going out of his way to threaten James.

"Should I tell Patterson?"

"I don't know what good it would do," Tom answered.

James felt that the ghost of Bloody Knuckles was loose and coming to haunt him. He turned over the name of every person he knew in his mind, anyone who knew he was even on the expedition. He couldn't imagine who would send this to him. As the group readied itself to get back on the trail, James could hear the screams of Bloody Knuckles ringing in his ears. Would he ever forget?

~ *Chapter 19* ~

FORGIVENESS

That night, Alice curled up next to Star Eye in their wickiup. Red still hadn't returned to camp. One of the women was snoring loudly. Alice looked at the logs lying on top of each other, the smell of wood all around her. She thought of the lullabies her mother would sing to her at night to make her feel safe. She petted Star Eye between his ears on the top of his head and he rolled over to get his belly rubbed. *I wonder if anyone ever sang to Red to put him to sleep,* she pondered. Alice started humming to herself and to Star Eye, remembering tunes that came from a place so very far away from where she was now. Suddenly, all of her anger toward Red started to turn to worry. *I can't believe that he*

hasn't come back yet, she thought. *He doesn't have his gun or anything.* An owl hooted outside. *Protect him, Owl,* she urged. But she was not reassured.

The whole night passed and Red did not return. In the morning, the clan was loading the dog sleds and Alice looked around hopefully. She even tried to stall, but she knew they couldn't wait very long. *What would life be like with the Sheepeaters if Red wasn't here?* Alice wondered. Even though they hadn't spoken since joining the tribe, his familiar presence was comforting to her in these new surroundings. She let out a cough as she roped a digging stick to the dog sled. The morning air always made her lungs feel tight. It often hurt to take deep breaths, so she didn't even try anymore. Green Blossom looked over in Alice's direction and smiled supportively, looking concerned about her cough. Suddenly, Alice's life with the Sheepeaters felt permanent. *If Red is gone,* she thought, *I don't know if I will ever leave. Will I see my family again?*

"There!" Green Blossom's little brother pointed to the brush. Red was walking steadily toward the group. The sun was beginning to glow orange over the mountains, and the birds were chirping in a chorus as they greeted the day. Red's eyes were sunken, his hair was caked with mud. He looked like he hadn't slept all night. Green Blossom's mother repeated her mantra to everyone in Shoshone, "We will continue as we were," and everyone lowered their heads and tried to concentrate on their tasks. *How can I continue with my task?* Alice thought. She wanted to run and hug him to make sure that he was okay. *Well, he ignored me for days so maybe he deserves it a little,* she thought. Red saw that they weren't paying any attention to him. His work dog ran over to greet him, but Green Blossom's cousin, Bear Heart, ordered the dog back. Red tried to join the group and put supplies on a dog sled, but Bear Heart edged him away. Red looked defeated.

"Let him help," Alice said suddenly to Bear Heart, stopping her work. Everyone heard and turned to look in her direction. Red sheepishly glanced at her for a brief moment and then lowered his eyes again. His hands were at his sides, hanging uselessly. Alice was surprised at her own willingness to help Red after his coldness, the hurtful things he'd said, and the scene he had created the day before. *Remember how much he helped you. Remember that he is like family to you now,* she felt in her heart. The rest of the clan eyed each other, but continued with their tasks. All was quiet. Bear Heart waited for a long while. He tightened a strap, stuffed clothing and tobacco into a satchel, and even sat for a moment to rest.

Of everyone in the clan, Bear Heart was the most hard-hearted about accepting Alice and Red into the group. He was particularly severe to Red. Red stood silently, rejected and vulnerable. Bear Heart looked over at the boy with intensity. He suddenly picked up a blanket and threw it at Red's chest, then continued with his tasks. Red caught the blanket with both arms and embraced it. It was a sign that he had been accepted. He was supposed to start packing, but he just stood there, his face hidden in the cloth, his shoulders shaking.

Alice was about to put her things down to go console him, but Green Blossom shook her head no. Alice thought of how Red had carried her through the fire, shared food with her, and had chosen to take this journey to protect her. Finally, Red lifted his head, and wiped away his tears. *Were they tears of joy? Sadness? Relief?* Alice wondered. Red purposefully went over to his belongings and picked up his precious gun.

"I'm leaving this here," he announced to everyone,

even though they were trying to ignore him. He threw the gun into the woods. It was his way of saying that he would work with their ways. It was his way of making up for the broken bow. *I can't believe he gave up his gun,* Alice thought. Her heart ached for the sacrifice Red had just made. She knew what that meant to him. Discarding the gun was as if he were throwing away a piece of himself—a rotten piece, but a piece of himself nonetheless.

As the group finished packing up, out of the corner of her eye Alice saw Bear Heart walk over to the gun when Red was not looking. Bear Heart looked at the gun with a thin smile on his face and quickly hid it in a blanket. He marched back to the group and affixed the gun to his dog sled. Everyone was pre-occupied with the departure and didn't seem to notice Bear Heart's behavior. Or if they did, they didn't care.

~ *Chapter 20* ~
YELLOWSTONE LAKE

James decided to tell Patterson about the *Long Live Bloody Knuckles* note after all. There was nothing the soldier could do but reassure James that he was there to protect him. Patterson put a steady hand on James' shoulder and James felt comforted. It was exactly what he needed.

Tom was once again a dutiful friend, eager to distract James with all the wonders around them. It wasn't difficult, because the mud volcanoes were on the edge of another beautiful site: Yellowstone Lake. It was a vast, dark blue, tranquil lake that contrasted with the bright colors and violent nature of the hot springs. There was a small, low island in the lake where hundreds of brown and white geese were amassed.

Mr. Blackmore and a few others went fishing in the lake, then cooked their fish in a nearby hot spring. James and Tom followed suit and found the whole process practical and funny at the same time. They could even spot more hot springs just under the surface of the lake. James had seen all kinds of springs and geysers along their journey. He had seen yellow springs, bright blue springs, bubbling mud springs, big springs that were like lakes, and some that were tiny, deep holes. Some were flat all around except for a bubbling center, but he hadn't seen any yet that were under another body of water. This amazed him. Dr. Hayden and Mr. Blackmore saw James goggling at the scene and came up to give him a pat on the back.

"Dr. Hayden! Greetings, sir." James said. He couldn't hide his enthusiasm for the man. "Greetings, Mr. Blackmore." *Two of the heroes of Yellowstone! And well-connected to politicians,* James thought.

"How is the adventure so far, boy? You holding up? Writing letters to Congressman McCormick?" Dr. Hayden asked.

"Oh, yes sir. It is such an honor to be here. Yes." James had forgotten that he had used his relative's clout to get on the trip in the first place. He quickly changed the subject. "These are such strange formations. I never imagined a hot spring or a geyser under a lake."

"The best geysers are yet to come," Dr. Hayden said with a smile. "Do you know the difference between a geyser and hot spring?" Dr. Hayden asked. In fact, Tom had explained it to James a few times, but it never stuck in his head.

"No, sir," James answered, eager-eyed.

"Well, son, these are all geothermal features."

"'Geo,' like geology?" James asked.

"That's right. Or geography. 'Geo' is anything of or relating to the earth. And thermal is anything of or relating to heat."

"Like a thermometer?" James asked.

"Somewhat, yes. So geothermal is like the heat of the earth. Please stop me if you've learned any of this at school. I'm sure a boy your age knows far more than I assume." James remembered how he had lied about his age to get on the expedition. He decided it was probably best to stop asking questions and just listen to what the doctor had to say so he wouldn't give away his age.

"No sir. And it's always most interesting and more thorough to hear it from a professional like you."

Hayden accepted the flattery warmly.

"To put it plainly, a geyser is a hot spring under pressure that boils to the point of explosion."

"Thank you, sir. That is much clearer now." James tried to sound as professional as possible.

"Any time, son. I'm glad that you are able to learn something along the way while looking for your beloved sister. We are glad that the size of our group has provided ample protection for you thus far. Any luck?" Hayden inquired.

James' smile faded.

"Not really," he answered.

"Well, keep up the good work. I'm sure you'll find everything you're looking for. We are happy to have you as general assistants. Your friend Tom has been especially helpful to Dr. Peale."

"I'll tell him you said so," James said proudly.

Mr. Blackmore peered across the grand, blue lake.

"I find this suitable for Indian encampment and likely to furnish Indian remains," Mr. Blackmore said. "I am going to investigate."

"Excellent. I am going to collect some more specimens. James, would you like to join?" Hayden asked.

James was thrilled to be invited, but his bones ached from all the exploring. The discussion of Alice made him desire some time alone, and something about the lake was calling to him. Maybe it was the tranquility of the blue waters.

"I am waiting for Tom to come back from an excursion with Dr. Peale," James said.

"Excellent. Well, carry on," Hayden encouraged. "We understand loyal friendships." Dr. Hayden and Mr. Blackmore exchanged a confident look of old comrades, then went their respective ways.

James sighed and reached into his satchel to pull out his compass for inspiration. It indicated that he was facing southeast, but otherwise gave him no comfort. He rested his hand against a tree and stared out at the water, lost in thought.

A few times, he thought he spotted movement across the lake. He strained his eyes to see, but it turned out to be a crane or a gull or a swallow. *Wishful thinking,* he frowned. *What are the chances that I would actually find Alice here, now? She could be anywhere ... if she's even still alive.*

Chapter 21

ON THE OTHER SIDE

By the time they arrived at their camp near Yellowstone Lake, Red had made an earnest attempt to be helpful. This camp near the lake was a more permanent location that the Sheepeaters used over and over, so they had wickiups already established by some caves, as well as stone bowls that had been left there for future use. Red, Alice, Green Blossom, and her sister decided to walk down to look at the lake.

After seeing spewing geysers, the Grand Canyon of the Yellowstone, marshes and trees, and all varying kinds of nature, Alice now saw what she considered the crown jewel: Yellowstone Lake. All of her worried thoughts about getting home to her family melted away at the sight of the shimmering waters and the cleansing winds.

"Why didn't we make our camp closer to the water?" Red asked Green Blossom.

"We decide not to make camp too close to lake because of white visitors and other Indian enemies. Better to stay higher up. Away," Green Blossom answered.

"Well, this looks like a better spot," Red claimed. His dog pranced beside him obediently. Alice looked down at Star Eye, happy with how her training had been going. There were ripe berries everywhere and everything was in full bloom. Alice felt as happy as the yellow flowers all around her. Across the lake to the west, Alice could see the slightest hint of fall colors in the trees and the lower vegetation.

Alice left the group and wandered down to the lake with Star Eye to fully enjoy the splendor of the scenery in solitude. She climbed up a small ridge in between some trees, and arrived at a small clearing by the edge of the water.

"Sit," she said to Star Eye, who quickly obeyed. She looked out over the lake and became lost in thought. *I feel different when I look at something beautiful like this,* she contemplated. *I don't know why, but it makes me feel closer to everything that ever was and will be.* Alice thought of the Sheepeaters' belief in water people, or what they called *pandozoavits.* Alice was half-expecting one of the squat, heavy, ghostlike creatures to pay her a visit. She knew the spirits were strongest in the mountains, but there was something about this lake that called to her.

Suddenly Star Eye shot up at the sound of footsteps nearby. Alice looked up and saw Red approaching. They hadn't been alone together since their escape from Slinger and Farley and their misadventures in the woods.

Red bent down and petted Star Eye between his ears, then came and sat next to Alice and ordered his dog to sit. They reposed on the edge of the lake for a while, looking at the glistening water below them.

Alice thought of James and Tom, and how much they would love to see the falls and geysers and the beautiful lake. She wished there was a magical horse with wings that could fly her over all of Yellowstone, all the way over the hot springs and back to Bozeman. She would get her whole family and they would each ride their own winged horse, each one a different color, through the clouds and around the mountains. She would bring them all to this very spot, and they would have a picnic of Mattie's delicious apple pie and then ...

"You're daydreaming," Red said.

"No I'm not."

"Yes you are."

Alice and Red sat in silence again. Alice looked down at her wristband, and twirled it, annoyed that she was stuck in such a beautiful place with Red, the strange one. *What did he come over here for anyway?* She wondered. She noticed Red looking at her wristband so she stopped twirling it and looked away.

"It's okay to daydream," Red said to Alice.

"I know it is."

"Okay."

"Well, I don't want to talk about it." She was trying to be a good person, but it was so hard with Red sometimes. It was like trying to hug a porcupine.

"I sometimes daydream about my mom," Red said. Alice was taken by surprise. She had only seen Red with his dad, Bloody Knuckles. Red seemed like a motherless person to her; it was hard to imagine him receiving any kind of tenderness. She had heard rumors back in Miles' shop at the newspaper office that Red had killed his mother, but that seemed ridiculous. *Or was it?*

"My mom, she was hurt real bad and then was never the same again."

"Oh, I'm sorry," Alice said. "What happened?" she asked, even though she wasn't quite sure she wanted to know.

"My dad said Indians shot her, but I don't know. When he had too much whiskey, he did bad things. Very bad things. He did bad things to me, too. He was a rotten man, Alice," Red said. She didn't say anything. She was worried for a minute that Red might cry again, like that terrible moment when he had buried his face in the blanket and discarded his gun.

"Well, enough about her. She is a survivor, I'll tell you that much. Even after my father took me and abandoned her, she figured out how to get to us—in all ways." Red let out a little laugh, which was strange because it wasn't funny. It was more of a sad laugh. But still, it was the first time she'd ever heard him laugh at all.

"You had a really nice family," Red said. Alice felt uncomfortable. "It seemed like they genuinely cared about you," he continued. *Is he a little envious of me, and I never knew it?* Alice wondered.

"I hope they still do," Alice said, troubled by the past tense of Red's words.

"Of course they do," Red said definitively. "But me . . ." he trailed off. "There's too many things that I know, Alice." He looked troubled. *Do I really want to know the things he knows?* Alice wondered. "I know too much about people and places," Red said. "The bad things that they do." Alice just nodded her head, amazed at Red's newfound openness.

"Anyway, I know that you're younger than me and all, but I just wanted to say thank you," Red said. Now Alice was completely surprised. "Thank you for . . ." Red started to elaborate, but the moment was interrupted by Green Blossom and Smiles Like Chipmunk, who ran over to them out of breath.

"We must go back to camp. There are white men across the lake. It is too dangerous for us. We will leave immediately tomorrow morning," Green Blossom declared.

"Let's go," Red said strongly. As they ran back to camp with their dogs, feathers dangling from their hair, Alice realized that she could very well be running away from friends or even troops from Fort Ellis that were looking for her. But she kept running, wheezing, through the fire in her lungs and through the fire in her mind. She thought about Red's words. *I wonder what Red was going to thank me for,* she thought. *I wonder what else he would have said.* She kept running, glancing back over her shoulder.

That night, Alice woke Red from his sleep.

"What do you want?" he growled, having lost all of his earlier pleasantness.

"Red," Alice whispered, trying not to wake the cousins in his wickiup. "This may be our chance to go home. We won't put the tribe in danger if you and I can go alone. We can pack up tonight. Let's wake up Green Blossom and take the most basic provisions and go quietly."

"I am awake," Green Blossom said, following Alice into the wickiup where Red was sleeping. A few of the cousins stirred. *Oh no,* Alice thought.

Green Blossom put up her hand to calm Alice.

"I followed you because I knew what was to happen. I will help if you want to go. You are free to stay or to leave from us as you wish," Green Blossom said. "I will tell Standing Rock and we will help." Alice was so relieved. She went over and hugged her sister. But Red was not smiling. He sat up from under his robes.

"Alice, that could easily be Farley and Slinger again. We don't know." Alice hadn't considered this.

"I think we should stay for a little longer," Red whispered. Bear Heart turned over and covered his ears. Red continued. "We will have other chances to go if we want. But this seems too dangerous."

Alice bit her lip and considered her options. She looked to Green Blossom.

"This is your decision. We cannot go back because it is too risky. The white man will capture us and send us to a reservation. We can give what you need to go," she said. A wolf howled outside. Alice considered being alone with Red again in the wilderness, possibly even walking back into the hands of their enemies. Her stomach turned into a knot.

"Maybe we should stay for a little longer," she said. "Just a little longer." Little did she know that it was her brother James who was just across the lake.

Chapter 22

CROSSING PATHS

The Hayden Expedition left Yellowstone Lake and headed to the Lower Geyser Basin. There, the Northern Division of the expedition united with the Southern Division, also known as the Snake River Division. The meeting point was named Camp Reunion. It looked like a village of scruffy men, dogs, and donkeys. The meeting had all been part of the expedition plan, but there was still a degree of amazement that the reunion had actually worked. The group doubled in size and the noise doubled in volume. Conversations and greetings abounded, infusing the ethereal Geyser Basin with an unusual degree of humanity.

James was quickly distracted by the stories of comrades from the Snake River Division who had made their way through the Teton Mountains. There was a rumor that two members of the expedition, including Mr. Langford, had actually reached the summit of the Grand Teton! James tried to keep a special eye out for Mr. Langford, the superintendent of the park. James didn't know what it meant to be an "intendent" of something. He didn't even think that it was a real word. *The closest thing is to intend,* James thought. *Maybe he really intends to do something great with the park, and that's what makes him a superintendent.* At least that's what James hoped.

There was a big celebration as Hayden assembled all sixty men together and made an encouraging speech. He named the British guest Mr. Blackmore, the painter Thomas Moran, and Superintendent Nathaniel Langford honorary members of the U.S. Geological Survey. Everyone threw their hats in the air and applauded enthusiastically.

James stared at Langford during Hayden's speech. The superintendent had a bandana tied around his neck and a thin smile on his face. He didn't seem to be a casual man, and James found this promising. His nose was as straight as his dark beard, and the two seemed to jut forward together, like a pointy elbow. *The first superintendent!* James could barely contain himself. Equally as exciting, Langford had brought his nephew Spencer along on the trip. Spencer looked to be about seventeen, and enthusiasm beamed from his lightly bearded face. There was another seventeen-year-old on the expedition who James quickly realized was Mr. Blackmore's nephew. The relatives embraced in a hearty reunion. While the rest of the men were gathering and exchanging tales of adventure, Tom quickly assembled the new list of people from the Snake River Division in his journal.

Southern Division of the Hayden Expedition
U.S. Geological Survey of the Territories

James Stevenson, Director
Professor Frank H. Bradley, Chief Geologist,
 from Knoxville, TN
W. R. Taggart. Asst. Geologist
Gustavus R. Bechler, Chief Topographer
Rudolph Hering (Herring?), Asst. Topographer,
 from Fairmount Park, Philadelphia
Thomas W. Jaycox, Asst. Topographer

William Nicholson, Meteorologist
John M. Coulter, Botanist
Dr. Josiah Curtis, Surgeon and Microscopist
    from Boston
C. Hart Merriam, Ornithologist
Campbell Carrington, Naturalist
William H. Jackson, Photographer ✱
Charles R. Campbell, Asst. Photographer
Robert Adams, General Asst.
P. J. Beveridge. General Asst.
J. S. Negley. General Asst.
W. A. West, General Asst.
Sidford F. Hamp, Guest, Age Seventeen,
    Nephew of William Blackmore ✱

    J. B. Brown, General Asst.
    J. C. Jones, General Asst.
Hon. Nathaniel P. Langford, Guest ✱
C. S. Spencer, Guest, Age Seventeen,
    Nephew of Nathaniel P. Langford
    Dr. Reagles, Guest
"Beaver Dick" Leigh, Guide,
    old trapper who settled with
    Indian woman named Jenny.

When they were away from the crowd, James and Tom sat by a hot spring and exchanged stories they'd heard. Tom had captured a few bugs and they sloshed around in a jar of alcohol preservative.

"I heard the Tetons are stupendous," James said.

"You know what the name means, right?" Tom added. James shook his head.

"It's French for the big ... you know," Tom held out his hands in front of his chest. They laughed and shared a mutual appreciation for the crudeness of the early trappers. Tom always had a way of seeing the profane side of life and making it seem grandly hilarious. In that way, he fit right in with the mountain men.

"Maybe the new men know something about Grizzly Ranch," James said. "Maybe I'll interview some of them."

"Okay," Tom said. "Quick game. If you had to pick one guy from the expedition to be lost in the woods with for a week, who would you pick? Would you choose a mountain man like Beaver Dick, Bill Hamilton, or that crazy Scottish guy we met back at the mining camp?" James considered. "Or would you get chummy with a wealthy British guy like Blackmore, who knows a lot about Indians and is well connected in Washington?"

James considered this as well. "Or would you want to be with one of the scientists like Dr. Hayden or Dr. Peale?"

"You forgot Langford, the park's new superinten-dent," James added.

"Okay, or him," Tom said.

"And Crissman, the photographer."

"What help would he be if you were lost?"

"Good point," James said. His train of thought stopped as he spotted some figures moving amidst the steam a short distance away. *It can't be,* he thought to himself. He saw the distinct strut of a bulky man, lumbering through the woods, his large knife holstered to his side. Trailing behind him was a lanky, goofy-looking man with an overbite and bullets in an am-munition belt cascading down his front. James craned his neck through the steam, which puffed around aim-lessly at the whim of the wind. *Is it really them?*

"James ... James!" Tom snapped his fingers in his friend's face.

"Shhhhhh!" James cautioned, shaking off the vision. The two men heard James' name being called and looked around for a moment. James slunk down behind the steam and tried to pull Tom down with him.

"I don't know why you're making that big of a deal out of it. It's not that hard of a question. I could tell you who I would rather be lost with in the wild. I would pick ... " Tom started in.

"Not now, Tom," James hushed.

"Everything okay? What are you staring at?" Tom asked.

"Do you see those men over there? I'm not imagining them, right?"

"Sure, I see them," Tom said standing up on the rock.

"No! Don't stand," James panicked.

"Alright. You want me to call them over?" Tom said, alarmed by James' behavior.

"No, definitely not. But you see them?"

"Sure. Real mean-looking pair," Tom observed. "Wait a minute ... I recognize those buffoons. Is that... "

"Steel-Fist Farley and Charley Slinger of the Long Coat Gang," James finished Tom's sentence. James' breathing quickened. He couldn't let the men see him. *Maybe they're coming for me, to exact revenge for the death of Bloody Knuckles,* he feared.

He slunk further and further toward the earth, down the side of the rock, until he was sitting in the lichen by the spring. *Maybe they know something about Alice,* he wondered. He focused on the steaming water and the small bacteria that lived around it, bringing out the spring's beautiful colors. He was trying to distract himself from the presence of these thugs, but his head filled with Bloody Knuckles' dying shrieks of pain. All else fell silent.

As soon as the men were gone, Tom and James immediately ran to get Patterson and alert him to the presence of Farley and Slinger, who had been Bloody Knuckles' thugs. Patterson told the boys to make camp a little distance away from the rest of the expedition that night. Chen joined them heartily, his own curiosity about these two boys continuing to escalate. James was glad for Chen's company, if something should occur.

"It's not suspicious that I'm here for the government, as a soldier, so I will look into matters. You lay low," Patterson said, and nobly went back to camp with the rest of the men.

Before they went to sleep that night, James looked around the Lower Geyser Basin. *This is like my dream,* he thought. *The way the geysers are all steaming on the* side of the hill, exploding in tandem with each other. James looked at the mystical scene. *And the two ghoulish men, running after me ... Charley Slinger and Steel-Fist Farley ...* James tried to remember. *My compass,* he thought, and reached into his satchel to feel it.

James had a restless sleep. He kept turning over the letter he got from Bozeman in his head, *"Long Live Bloody Knuckles!"* George's red face and large red nose were floating in front of him at the mines, his lips slowly mouthing *Grizzly Ranch, Grizzly Ranch, Grizzly Ranch ...*

"James," Tom said.

"What?"

"You're talking in your sleep."

"Oh, sorry," James said.

"S'okay."

James shivered and pulled his blankets up. It was a moonless sky covered with a layer of clouds as thick as the thoughts muddling James' mind.

The next morning, Patterson came riding to their camp as Chen prepared breakfast and Tom tried to light a fire. *Maybe we can figure out how to get*

Patterson to ask the Long Coat Gang about Alice. They have to know something. They disappeared at the same time she disappeared. They might have clues. Then a terrible realization crossed James' mind. *What if they killed her?* James gulped. He considered, for a moment, that maybe ignorance was better. He shook it off. *It's best to know.*

But answers weren't going to come soon.

"All clear. The men must have left," Patterson said riding into camp.

"What did you see?" Tom asked.

"I think they were trying to stay hidden. They put up camp a far ways out. I followed them secretly. It seemed like they were up to no good; Farley was sharpening his knife," Patterson observed. *He always did that back at Mammoth Hot Springs,* James recalled. "They went into a tent to meet with another group or a person, but I couldn't see beyond that."

James looked at Patterson with great appreciation. The idea that he worked for the military and that the purpose of his station near Bozeman was for protection reassured James tremendously.

"But they're gone now?" James asked, slightly disappointed that they wouldn't be able to glean more information from the terrible two.

"Yes, as far as I can tell, they've left the area completely," Patterson replied.

Who were they were talking to? James wondered.

"Bad, bad," Chen said.

"They are pretty bad," Tom agreed.

Chen started shaking his head from side to side, and kept saying, "Bad, bad," as he took a pot off the fire. James couldn't help but think there was more to Chen's words.

Chapter 23

THE HUNT

The Sheepeater clan left Yellowstone Lake and made for higher ground in the Absaroka Mountains. Alice questioned whether or not she had made the right decision by leaving the lake, but concluded that she could not have gone on without Red. *He should have wanted to go with me,* Alice mulled.

Once they had reached higher ground, the clan set up camp and was able to sleep more peacefully. Alice and Green Blossom were growing closer as the days passed. More and more, she felt she had a real sister. One morning, Alice awoke to Green Blossom smiling in her face.

"There is a big hunt today," Green Blossom said

excitedly. "Let us watch in secret."

After the girls quickly dressed, Green Blossom grabbed Alice's hand and they ran up to the top of a red cliff overlooking an open valley. There were tufts of sagebrush dotting the landscape and the earth below turned a dusty, whitish brown. There weren't very many trees.

"Do not tell sister or mother I do this," Green Blossom said. "They say it bring bad spirits. But I do not think so. We bring good spirits," she said, her green eyes sparkling.

Alice and Green Blossom squirmed on their bellies to the edge of the bluff and positioned themselves

behind a jutting rock. Alice's stomach dropped when she looked down. Her legs started to shake, but she reminded herself to stay strong. Having Green Blossom there helped her remain calm.

"Look, there is Boy Who Breaks Bows," Green Blossom cheered, interrupting Alice's thoughts. It was Red, all dressed up for the hunt and talking to the rest of the men. "He is strong."

Strong? Alice was taken aback.

"You are too hard to him," Green Blossom asserted, reading Alice's face.

"No I am not!" Alice said, defensively. "You just don't know him," she snapped. Green Blossom raised her eyebrows but chose to drop the subject. *He has been nicer lately,* Alice reconsidered upon a moment of reflection. *Maybe I am angry at him for not taking the risk to go home.*

The catch pen was an amazing construction, made out of large pieces of logs, tree trunks, rocks, and brush. Green Blossom explained that the men made the pen blend in with the landscape to help trap the sheep. They watched below as the men finished putting logs and sticks into the a horseshoe-shaped structure. Alice saw Bear Heart and wondered where he was hiding

Red's gun, and if he had the gall to bring it on the hunt, but she didn't see any sign of it. *Not that he has bullets for it anyway,* she thought.

The sheep were grazing nearby, seemingly content and oblivious to their impending doom. Every once in a while, a sheep sensed a threat and went into alarm posture. It raised its head and held it rigidly while backing away from the situation. Then the hunt was put in motion.

The dogs started to round up the sheep. The men stood by, attentively, with their bows, quiet and patient.

"Listen," Green Blossom whispered. Alice could hear Spotted Eagle singing from his spot in the catch pen to lure the sheep in. The sheep ran away from the dogs and up the log ramp.

"Look, it's working!" Alice exclaimed, getting into the thrill of the hunt. The sheep ran up the ramp, and once they were in the enclosure of logs they couldn't get out. That's when Alice saw one of the men run toward an animal with a big stone in his hand.

"I can't watch." Alice winced and curled up under the brush. She heard the sounds of the panicked sheep. She covered her ears and closed her eyes and waited.

"It is over," Green Blossom said, poking Alice. Alice lifted her head to look at the scene below. There were three sheep lying dead in the pen. The men let out a big cheer and started to dance around. Red was not sure what to do, so he just stood there awkwardly.

"We have much food and work to do now," Green Blossom said excitedly.

"What are they doing with that sheep head?" Alice asked and let out a little cough and a shudder at the gruesome scene.

"We leave skull as offering to the Gods. Because then the spirit of the sheep will return to the rocks or be in the trees." The Sheepeater Indians looked at their environment in a way Alice had never before imagined. They didn't distinguish between what was in the real world and what was in the spirit world. Alice took to this philosophy immediately because it infused everything in the natural world with meaning and made it holy. They thought plants and inanimate objects had souls; trees had spirits, so did mountains and rocks. It was very different than the world in which she was brought up. She looked at her wristband and thought of her pledge. *It seems so much easier for them to respect the animals,* Alice thought, *even when they hunt.*

Green Blossom caught Alice looking at the tattered piece of string wrapped around her wrist.

"It is about animals? I see you look when animal is hurt or killed."

"Kind of," Alice said. "Me, my friend Tom, and my brother—not Red, my brother James—we made a serious promise to each other to protect the animals and the park and the nature in it. And its people, like you. Each of us agreed to wear this wristband as a symbol to remind us of our vows and give us courage to act." Alice felt noble for her promise.

Green Blossom looked at Alice. "What is park?" she asked innocently. *Of course she wouldn't think of this as a park*, Alice thought. *This is her home. She probably doesn't know what a city park is, let alone a new idea like a national park.*

"Well, a huge piece of land was put aside by the government, I think—larger than some states back East where I was born," Alice tried to explain. "It's supposed to be a natural place for people to enjoy."

"Isn't all around us natural?" Green Blossom asked.

"I guess," Alice replied. It was difficult to explain that her land wasn't being taken for people to live in, but to be set aside as a natural wonderland. It was different from other parks in that way, too.

"How do you know where is this park?" Green Blossom asked.

"People write it on a map," Alice posited, unsure of the answer. There wasn't a fence around the park and it was enormous. It was hard to say exactly where it started and ended.

"Do the animals know they should stay in this park or go outside of it?" Green Blossom laughed.

"I guess not," Alice said, feeling a little ridiculous.

Green Blossom became suddenly serious. Her dark hair was resting in the dirt, her green eyes sparkling against the blue sky and the dusty sagebrush. *I hope I didn't offend her,* Alice worried.

"I do not know about this park, or ways of white people, but I would like to make this promise, too," Green Blossom said definitively. She had a look of determination.

"Really?" Alice questioned.

"I want to protect the nature and the animals and my people, too." Green Blossom sensed the importance of Alice's efforts and inspected the piece of cloth tied on her wrist.

"Okay," Alice became animated. "We will do a

ceremony and you will take the pledge," Alice said, liking the idea of a ritual.

"This is good," Green Blossom stated. "Let us do this soon. Now we go and celebrate success of great hunt."

They crept back off the side of the mountain, making sure none of the men would see them, and sprinted gleefully back to camp.

Chapter 24

OLD FAITHFUL

Without any more leads about Farley and Slinger, Patterson, Chen, Tom, and James headed back to join the raucous group of sixty men.

"Where did you fellows go off to?" Bill Hamilton, the mountain man, came strutting over happily. "The whole group took a grand picture together. Mr. Jackson set it up. I'm sorry you missed it."

"Well, I guess we won't end up in any of the official records," Tom sulked.

"That's okay," James said, a bit disappointed, but still fearful about Bloody Knuckles' men. "It doesn't really matter. What's most important to me is to find my sister," James said to Hamilton.

"I thought you just made all that up to get on the expedition, but you keep talkin' about it, so either you're lost in your own lie or it's true," Hamilton said. Then he let out a short laugh. "I hope for your sake you're lost in your own lie because looking for a person out here would be darn near impossible."

James thought about it for a moment and then realized how ridiculously daunting this undertaking was, after all.

"I suppose it does seem impossible," James answered, troubled.

The large group photo had marked the end of the massive gathering of the divisions. Soon, groups began to disband. Mr. Blackmore would depart with a large party, ready to get back to England. The main scientists of the Southern Division would continue down to the Tetons from the East Side toward Jackson's Hole. A section of the Southern Division, including superintendent Langford and photographer William Henry Jackson, would go back through Mammoth Hot Springs.

James thought of McCartney and Horr and their makeshift hotel. It suddenly seemed luxurious in comparison to the unending nights outside in the frost.

I'd like to see how everyone is doing there before I head up to Bozeman, James thought. James conferred with Patterson and they agreed that a stop back through Mammoth would be the best route to take on a search for Alice.

After Mr. Blackmore's group departed, Hayden was the next to leave the Upper Geyser Basin with the Northern Division, heading west out of the park toward Virginia City. James, Tom, Patterson, and Chen made a collective stop with Dr. Peale for collecting specimens and exploring.

"The geysers are named as follows," Tom said, looking down at the basin and consulting his diary. "Old Faithful, Bee Hive, Giantess, Castle, Grand, Turban, Saw-Mill, Giant, Grotto, the Riverside, the Fan, and the Soda Geyser. Those are the main ones that I have." After looking at them all, James thought most of the names accurately described the shape and feel of each geyser.

James imagined that the surface of the moon must look like the Upper Geyser Basin area of Yellowstone. The earth in the geyser basin was bald and white. There were patches where it looked like it was bleeding orange as the boiling water streamed down the sides of hills, picking up bacteria along the way. The edges of the geyser basins were ornamented with bead-like silica.

The group spent a whole day dedicated entirely to Old Faithful. At this point, Dr. Peale needed some extra help. They tried to figure out the depth of the geyser tube of Old Faithful, but every time they let down the entire length of their rope, 360 feet, and then withdrew it, the end was completely tangled. It happened every single time.

"This is impossible!" Dr. Peale declared. They tried to get the temperature of the water, but immediately after the eruption, the water sank out of sight and into the depths. Other times there was so much steam escaping that they couldn't even look into the tube.

"It looks like Old Faithful does not want to be studied, just admired," Tom commented.

"This is now officially my favorite spot in the park," James said.

"I'm still loyal to our secret meeting spot tree back at Mammoth," Tom said without hesitation.

"No way, this is far more curious," James insisted.

"Not true! Our tree is a piece of petrified wood. It is wood that was turned into stone by all of the mineral deposits. And it's not standing straight up, which is strange because the other trees are all standing upright.

And it shows different eras in Earth's history because you can look at all of its rings."

"Okay, okay," James surrendered. "But I still think this is more amazing."

James stood with his mouth agape, his head tilted back, staring at the shooting water. It wasn't as impressive in size, height, or oddness as some of the other geysers, but its regularity was astounding. James thought there must have been some sort of clock attached to it because it was so regular. He could gauge what time of day it was just based on its eruption schedule.

"It's like the heartbeat of Yellowstone," James said.

"That's why it's called Old Faithful, chum," retorted Tom, fondly punching James in the arm.

Everyone in the world should be able to see this, James thought to himself. *I must get back to Bozeman. I must carry on with our goal to protect this park, even without Alice. If we can't find her, I'll do it in her honor.* He looked down at his wristband and felt his eyes well up with tears, but he shook them away with his new-found sense of purpose.

~ *Chapter 25* ~

GAINING CONFIDENCE

The big sheep hunt was only the beginning of Red's success in hunting. He was getting better and better every day, gaining confidence, and feeling respected. This day would be no different.

It was hot in the late August sun at noon. From a distance, Alice saw Red and the other men entering the camp. The women went to greet the hunters and Alice quickly noticed that Red walked into the Sheepeater camp with a huge grin on his face. It was the first genuine smile Alice had seen on his freckled face since they had arrived. The men were murmuring amongst themselves. Red had helped set up a trap that caught many fish and then helped the men stave off a grizzly bear!

That night, everyone celebrated around a large fire, telling stories. It reminded Alice of her fun nights at Mammoth Hot Springs, animated faces laughing in the flickering light. She could only catch a few words of the stories, but it almost didn't matter. They were talking about Red's great feat with the grizzly bear. All of the young children were enraptured, and she enjoyed watching them giggle as much as anything else.

I can't believe it's the end of the summer already, Alice thought. *But it's amazing how much has happened in such a short time.* She sat back and petted Star Eye, feeling the warmth of friends. She and Red caught each other's eyes in the gathering, and he had a slight smile on his face. Alice felt a kind glow emanating from him and thought of their earlier conversation, how he had opened up about his mother and his struggles to overcome the past. Alice walked over to him and could feel Green Blossom watching out of the corner of her eye.

"Congratulations," she said to him.

"Thanks, Alice," Red said. "You have something in your hair." He reached over to pull off a huckleberry that had found its way into her mane. Alice felt uncomfortable again.

"You don't have to suddenly be so nice, you know,"

she said, probing. Red stepped away.

"Jealous?" he challenged.

"Of what?"

"Of my prized hunting skills," Red said proudly. "See, even Indians like to hunt, Alice. Everyone does." Alice's blood started to boil. *I knew he couldn't have changed so quickly.* She coughed and wheezed.

"But the difference is that people here hunt for food and not for fun," Alice said. Red was about to answer and then decided against it.

"Well, you've ruined the mood as usual," Red said and turned around. *Maybe it's better when we just don't talk,* Alice sulked. She turned and tried to take a deep breath, but it hurt.

Amidst the celebration of Red's big hunting success, Green Blossom's uncle, Spotted Eagle, stood before everyone and made an announcement in Shoshone. Alice and Red strained to understand it. Alice caught snippets of it; she was learning the language rather quickly. She heard "sun children" and "family," but that was all. Everyone nodded in agreement at what Spotted Eagle was saying, except for Bear Heart, who had a scowl on his face.

Green Blossom stood up to translate.

"We have decided," she began, "to have naming ceremony for Root Digger and Boy Who Breaks Bows, to make their Indian names official." Alice was overjoyed. She almost jumped up and hugged Green Blossom and the whole family. "But, we must make up for damage done by Boy Who Breaks Bows. We decided that he must make new wooden bow and arrow to replace the one he damaged. We will hold this ceremony after seven sleeps."

Red kept a stiff face. The tribe looked at him. Alice was nervous he might have another tantrum. She could almost feel his anger radiating through her own skin. Star Eye put his tail between his hind legs. *Maybe he can feel it too,* Alice thought.

But Red didn't have a tantrum. He didn't stand up and nod. He didn't bow. He didn't say yes. He didn't smile. He didn't cry. He just sat there, like a stone. Then he finally stood and cleared his throat.

"I will make a wooden bow, and then I want to go further. I want to make a sheep horn bow. I have seen these bows, and I ask for the help of any who want to show me how this is done."

He wants to make two bows? Alice was bewildered.

There were murmurings from the clan. A sheep horn bow took many months to complete.

"He is very strong," Green Blossom whispered to Alice. *Strongly conflicted,* Alice thought.

After what seemed like an hour of silence, Green Blossom's uncle responded in Shoshone, "So it is done," and the group prepared to leave camp. The next day, Alice saw Red studying the bows of all the men in camp. *Maybe he really is changing,* Alice considered.

~ *Chapter 26* ~
SHERIFF JAMES

Mammoth Hot Springs was bustling with activity when James, Tom, and their party from the Hayden Expedition returned. There were fifty tourists out enjoying the springs in addition to the government folk. Even though conditions were still rudimentary at the springs, it was luxurious compared to the wilderness they had just returned from and their long journey up from the Geyser Basins and Old Faithful.

Tom and James immediately returned to their meeting spot. It was where they had taken their original pledge with Alice to protect the park, and where they met, away from the grown-ups, to talk about important things. James was secretly hoping for some sign from Alice. After Mammoth Hot Springs, they would stop at Bottler's Ranch and then they would arrive in Bozeman. He was so close to seeing his parents that a knot of excitement was building up in his stomach. Now was his last chance to find any evidence and give his family hope that the journey had been worthwhile.

James and Tom walked up to their special spot, picked out for its beauty, seclusion, and the incredible petrified tree.

Tom let out an audible gasp.

"No!" he exclaimed.

Parts of Tom's favorite tree had been broken off and taken away. The tree had been a very attractive specimen, not only because it was gnarled and old, but also because it was part of a petrified forest. *Of course, this is something that tourists would want,* James thought furiously.

Tom went over and touched the dismembered tree. They were silent. James didn't know how to comfort his friend. Tom had been talking about the tree through-out their trip into the park, remaining loyal to it as his favorite feature. James thought he was maybe just being funny or stubborn. But that wasn't it. When they had first arrived earlier in the summer, Tom was the one who spotted it. Then the tree became the symbol of their pledge. *We couldn't even protect this tree,* James stewed, staring down, his cheeks blazing in frustration at his grimy wristband. Tom's favorite part of the whole park had been destroyed, and their pledge felt tarnished.

When they walked back to camp, Tom's head was hanging heavily. Suddenly, James started to notice changes in camp that had taken place in the short month that he was away. A few of the hot springs had been enlarged by human hands, and the edges of the terraces looked frayed.

"They're even cleaning their clothes in the hot springs," Tom muttered.

"Hey," James said. "Do you hear that?" It was laughter in the distance.

"Look over there, by the terraces." James pointed to another area of the hot springs below them to the right. One of the tourists was lugging an axe. There were a few of them, two men and two women.

"What are they doing?"

One of the women, in her full, long dress, dragged

the axe and then lifted it up over her head. It came down onto a sinter formation with a loud crack. Pieces went shattering to the ground. Some fell into hot springs and sizzled. James let out a gasp. Tom gulped. Their eyes were wide.

"What are those fools doing?" Tom cried.

"It looks like they're trying to take some of the formations back as souvenirs, like we tried to do," James said.

"Like you tried to do. Don't bring me into it," Tom snapped. James was embarrassed but he knew that Tom was particularly sensitive right now because of his tree. Earlier in the summer, James had tried to do exactly what the tourists were doing now. Then the wise railroad man Aldous Kruthers explained how the biggest profit was in bringing people to the untouched park, so it was in everybody's best interest to protect it.

"This is terrible," Tom said, looking at the people laughing and gathering up their souvenirs.

"How are we supposed to tell people this isn't a good thing to do?" Tom asked, skeptically.

"Can't we just say it?"

"Maybe, I guess." Tom seemed a little reluctant and broody. But James was determined. He had made his pledge to protect the park, and he was going to keep it. He couldn't stand what these new tourists had done to Tom's tree and to the terraces.

"Imagine what they would do to Old Faithful!" James huffed. He started to picture all the wonders that he had witnessed in the park—Tower Falls, the Upper and Lower Falls, Yellowstone Lake, all of the animals, geysers, hot springs—vandalized by irresponsible and greedy visitors. He started marching down the side of terraces, infuriated.

"Hello! You all—stop doing that! I want to talk to you!" he called out to the people below. They looked about trying to pinpoint the origins of the shouting. Once they spotted James' figure, they whispered to each other, trying to make out who it was.

"Come on, Tom. Let's go."

The boys had to go back and circle around a few of the terraces, but they finally made their way down to the group. James waved as they approached, but Tom lingered back a little.

"Hello!" James said and introduced himself again. He introduced Tom, too. "We just arrived with the government expedition. We're from Bozeman."

"Good afternoon." The group greeted James and

Tom warmly. "Would you like to join us? We've got some marvelous souvenirs in the making."

James laughed awkwardly.

"No, no. I actually wanted to talk to you about that." Everyone grew silent and attentive, the men putting hands up to their eyes to block the sun so they could get a better view of James. The women were content with their bonnets shading their eyes.

"Um," James looked back at Tom for support, but Tom seemed to be shrinking by the moment.

"Well, you see, these formations took a lot of years to form."

"You don't say," one of the women said mockingly. Everyone laughed.

"Yes, and they are worth a lot," James said angrily.

"We know, boy, that's why we're taking them."

"No! I mean, they're worth more when they're left alone."

"How's that?"

"Because everyone can come and see them, and they'll be protected."

"Well, we're here, boy, and they are worth something to us. So you can get off your high horse. Besides, we can take these pieces back so more people can see. Not very many people are going to be venturing down here any time soon." Everyone laughed.

"But ..." James wanted to explain to them that if everyone thought like that there wouldn't be any wonders left—that Yellowstone would be ruined, that each person was important in helping to keep the park intact—a beautiful land of curiosities. People would come to see it.

"But it's wrong," was all he could muster.

"It's wrong!" One of the women cackled. "Child, you don't know what you're talking about. This is the way of the world. We take a piece of sinter, it's ours. Just like the pieces of land that we have squatted as homesteaders are ours."

James thought for a moment. "This isn't a piece of your land. This is the government's property."

"Not if I have anything to say about it," one of the men mumbled under his breath.

"We all have a right to make money off of the land that's ours. Go tell that to your doctors and fancy men who have been taking specimens out of the park for years!" another man chimed in.

"That's for science," Tom said quietly behind James.

"What's the difference?" the man proposed.

"Looks like we have ourselves a Hot Spring Sheriff, everyone!" a woman shouted mockingly between her thin lips. "A Hot Spring Sheriff!" she called in a sing-song tone.

"There's no law in the territories, but apparently there is in this hellish, bubbling park!" the other woman encouraged her friend. Everyone laughed lightheartedly.

They're all just making fun of me, James cringed.

"And anyway, didn't the government put this land aside just *for* us? Well, I'm taking my piece." The woman bent down to take another hacked-off piece of sinter. "I'm going to send this one back East to my folks!"

"Well, that's the idea ... that if it's for all of us, then we should *all* be able to see it."

"No, the point is, honey, if it's for all of us, then I'm glad I got here first so I can get the best parts."

James was faltering. He didn't know how to talk to these people or to make them see things more clearly and less selfishly ... or actually, how it really was in their interests not to take pieces of the park.

"James, I think we have to get back to camp to

help with lunch. The hunters will be back soon," Tom piped in.

"That's right, listen to your friend. Skedaddle. You're ruining our fun!" They all let out nods of agreement. "We'll see you back at camp, Sheriff."

"Um, okay." James and Tom walked away in silence for a few moments and James could overhear them talking about him, even over the sounds of the cascading water.

"What a little runt."

"I think he's cute. So adorable, trying to protect his special hot springs."

James clenched his teeth and had his fists wound tightly at his sides. *I'm not cute.*

"Why didn't they take me seriously?" he barked at Tom when they had walked a little ways.

"Maybe because you're just a child."

"Maybe I'm young, but I'm not a child. I was right. They just didn't care what I had to say because they're old and narrow-minded. They don't realize that I am going to live longer than them, and that I'd like to have these formations around so that I can come back and look at them instead of a demolished hole in the ground! And why didn't you help me?" He stopped walking and turned to Tom.

Tom avoided James' wrath and looked away. He put his hands in his pockets.

"I knew it was trouble," Tom admitted.

"Well, why didn't you stop me?"

"You seemed pretty determined. I thought maybe I was wrong."

"Why did you think it was trouble?"

"Well, James, no offense, but you can't just walk up to people and tell them what they're doing is wrong. No matter how right you are."

"Why not?"

"It's kind of annoying. People don't like being lectured and told that they are behaving immorally, especially if they don't understand what you are talking about."

"This is ridiculous."

"And also, people will do whatever they think they can get away with."

"That's not true. Would you do whatever you think you can get away with?"

Tom considered for a moment.

"No."

"Would I? Would Mother? Would Jed? Would

Alice?" There was a pause of worry after the mention of her name. James felt a lump forming in his throat. He felt like he was failing at everything. *I can't protect the park, I can't find my sister, and now I'm yelling at my best friend.* He looked at his pledge bracelet and recalled how naïve and happy he had been with Tom and his sister, promising to take care of the animals and nature, and all of the people in the park.

"Calling it a national park is the easy part," James said quietly, fighting back tears.

"What do you mean?" Tom said.

"I don't know," James answered. But in his head he knew exactly what he meant. *Making promises is the easy part.*

Chapter 27

NAMING

The naming ceremony was one of the most exciting events Alice had ever experienced. The elders all gathered to bestow the names of "Root Digger" and "Boy Who Breaks Bows" on Alice and Red, who were dressed up in the softest of buckskins. Alice's hair was parted in the middle and a red line was drawn down her scalp. She looked over at her companion and suddenly felt the color was symbolic. She almost laughed seeing Red dressed head to toe in fancy Indian clothes.

Everyone from the tribe stood in line to give Red and Alice gifts. Alice received a dainty porcupine quill necklace from Green Blossom and Smiles Like Chipmunk. Her Indian mother, Standing Rock, gave her new moccasins for the winter. As she looked down at her tattered boots, she decided that nothing would have been more welcome. As each person came around with a gift, she realized how much she had grown to love every one of them. She not only called Standing Rock her mother in Shoshone, but she actually felt as if Standing Rock was another parent to her.

The two most memorable gifts were given to Red. First, Spotted Eagle stepped forward and presented Red with a walking stick. "This is for support when you feel lost and alone. You may think you are using it to lean on, but sometimes it will guide you," Green Blossom translated. Spotted Eagle had become Red's mentor. Alice could see this gift meant very much to him.

Next, Bear Heart walked up to Red and lowered his head. Alice recalled how Bear Heart wanted to leave Red alone in the wild after Red had broken the bow and arrow and fled.

As he approached Red, Bear Heart presented a gun. Not just any gun, Red's gun. Red was frozen still. It was hard to read what he was thinking. Green Blossom stepped up to translate.

"He says that he picked up gun after you threw it

on ground. Wanted it for himself," Green Blossom translated. "But he had powerful dream. He knew after dream that gun was for you and belonged with you. It was a memory from hunting spirits of how far you have come," Green Blossom said. Bear Heart stepped back and Red took the gun. Alice could see his eyes getting misty, but he held back the tears.

"Tell him that I have something for him, too," Red said, full of warrior pride. He bent down and uncovered a bow and arrow that had been resting under a sheepskin. Red had spent the week meticulously crafting the bow under the guidance of Spotted Eagle. It was sturdy and made from a chokecherry tree. He had used his sharp knife to scrape and smooth the back of the bow stave, but left the belly with the curve of the original wood. He bound the back with sinew for strength.

"I did not realize that you were the one who had made the bow that I had broken. Thanks to Green Blossom, I learned the truth." He looked at her and brightened.

"In making this, I learned the time and care it takes to make a bow. I am sorry that I broke your bow, brother. Even though this is the first one I ever made, and I trust my future bows will be much improved, I hope that you will accept this as a replacement." Bear Heart looked at Green Blossom as she translated.

"You are not Boy Who Breaks Bows, you are Man Who Makes Bows," Bear Heart said in Shoshone. Then he stepped forward and accepted his gift.

"Bow Maker!" Everyone cheered in Shoshone. The new names were given. Afterward, there was a big feast and celebration.

Amidst the dancing and festivities, Alice approached Bear Heart. A question was burning inside her. She brought Green Blossom over to translate.

"Tell him that was a very nice gift he gave to Red ... I mean, Bow Maker," Alice corrected. Green Blossom translated. Bear Heart nodded.

"I have a question," Alice said. She spoke slowly so that Green Blossom had time to relay the message. "When Red hunts, does he kill more animals than he can take with him? I mean, does he hunt the animals for fun and leave them there?" Alice asked, probing.

Bear Heart furrowed his brow and shook his head. Green Blossom translated. "He said that they only hunt what is of use to Sheepeaters. They do not leave dead animals for nothing," she said.

Alice nodded and smiled and thanked him again. As they walked away, Green Blossom was quiet. Alice was jangling from all of the new jewelry that she had received.

"Why did you ask this?" Green Blossom finally asked. "You do not trust your brother? You do not see his good?"

"You do?" Alice said, curious. Green Blossom blushed a little and looked away.

Chapter 28

A JOURNEY ENDS

The last sleep before they left for Bozeman was a restless one. James didn't feel he had even closed his eyes because his thoughts were racing through his mind like a herd of buffalo bolting from the hunt.

It was raining when the rest of the party woke up and Tom cursed because rain had seeped into his blankets. When he rolled over, he ended up in a pool of cold rainwater. Lighting a fire was near impossible, and no one could sit down without getting a wet mark on the seat of his trousers. By the time the party was ready to go, the rain had quit and the mountains were the regal rulers once again. Clouds formed around each of their peaks like ring-shaped crowns.

The men headed in the direction of Bozeman. With every passing moment, James felt he was turning away from where he was supposed to be. He could almost hear a voice calling him back to the trail to search for Alice. He also wanted to stay at Mammoth Hot Springs, to be there in person to protect its precious natural beauty. He cringed at the thought of more tourists arriving without a presence there to stop them from exploiting their surroundings. *I'll have to try and write something for Miles about this,* he thought.

"Come on, Chief, let's go talk to Patterson," James said to his horse. He rode up next to Patterson, finally having ample time to ask him questions.

"Greetings," Patterson said as he rode proudly on his horse.

"Um, I have a question," James said.

"Shoot," Patterson answered as he patted down his horse.

"What does the head of the park do? I mean, what is the job of the superintendent?"

"Honestly, I don't know. I was wondering the same thing myself."

"Oh." James was disappointed that there wasn't more to his answer.

"Don't look so upset. I didn't mean it like that. I know what I think he should do, but I'm not sure if that's what he's doing."

"Really? So you've noticed some ... problems?"

"I'll say. Some of these people here really need to learn how to clean up after themselves." James was so elated he couldn't contain himself. Here was a grown-up who actually saw some of the same problems that James was struggling to remedy.

"What do you mean?" James probed.

"Well, I am really concerned about the fires. People have to learn how to put them out, how to take care of them proper. Otherwise people will be responsible for too many forest fires in the park. We have the same issue back in Bozeman. But I can see it here, too."

"Huh." *I've never really thought of that one,* James pondered. He rubbed his chin. "What else?"

"Well, you and I both know the hunting is a problem." Patterson gave James a long, hard look. *Does he know about Bloody Knuckles?* James wondered. But then he realized Patterson didn't have to be talking about Bloody Knuckles. Bill Hamilton, the Bottler brothers, and every other tourist shot just about everything that moved in their path. When James went on short-distance searches for signs of Alice at Mammoth Hot Springs, almost every other day he would come across an animal carcass, shot but otherwise untouched. He expected people to hunt for food, but seeing dead, rotting animals everywhere was extremely unsettling.

"Did you notice how people are chopping apart the natural curiosities?" James asked.

"Yes. I also heard some rumors that you were trying to stop it."

"Uh ... yes." James was embarrassed. "I didn't execute that plan very well."

"At least you tried, James." Their horses shifted from side to side underneath them.

"How can we ... er, what can we do to really convince people?" James asked.

"I don't know if there's much we can do, given the circumstances," Patterson admitted. James was discouraged.

"But what I always do," the wise soldier went on, "is to make sure I am living by example. Sometimes telling people what to do all the time isn't as effective as just doing it right on your own. It's amazing how it can catch on."

"I suppose," James considered.

"You have to start small first, James." With this last piece of advice, James went over everything in his head and decided that he had made progress since his journey out to the park. He had taken a pledge. He realized that everything—the animals, the people, and nature—is interconnected.

"But what about the army? Why can't the army help protect the park?"

"In due time, James. In due time."

The party traveled seventeen miles and arrived in Bozeman just after noon. James and Tom said goodbye to all the men on the East Gallatin River before arriving in Bozeman proper. But it wasn't a full goodbye. Dr. Peale, Hayden, and a whole lot of them would be mooning around for a few weeks or months, finishing up their data collection in the area. James and Tom had already made plans with Crissman to visit his darkroom and see stereophotographs of the trip. James still couldn't believe that he had been in the company of such great men.

After Bill Hamilton tipped his hat and departed, Patterson gave James a rigid hug and a proud pat on the back.

"You were brave," Patterson commended. "I'll keep

my eyes and ears open for any news of this Grizzly Ranch. You let me know if anything else comes up. Get home safe." They exchanged one more embrace and then Patterson gallantly rode off and returned to Fort Ellis.

The last one to bid farewell was Chen. James approached and shook Chen's hand. Chen was only a few years older than James, but his skills in cooking, packing, cleaning, and mending were unmatched. His gap-toothed grin and young, tan face shone with optimism and eagerness. *I'll miss hearing his calls for breakfast,* James thought, *and his steady presence by my side.*

"Thanks for all of your help," James said. Chen nodded. A moment of understanding passed between them.

As James and Tom shook the hands of the men from whom they had learned so much, they knew it would be hard to go back to their lives as school boys under the roofs of their parents. They knew that they would never be the same. James turned to join Tom on the path home.

~ *Chapter 29* ~
AUTUMN

Alice tried to count the days since her departure from Mammoth Hot Springs and figured it was now early fall. The surroundings confirmed this. The bull elk were sparring and butting their antlers, competing for dominance in the mating season. There were grasshoppers everywhere. Down by the streams, the cutthroat trout were jumping to the surface for food. All of the animals seemed to be storing up for winter. Jays, grouse, and squirrels were all collecting seeds from the cones of pine trees. The Sheepeater tribe was doing the same, gathering provisions for the coming winter.

Spotted Eagle, Green Blossom's uncle, told Alice

that it was normal for her cough to be worse at this time of year. He said it was known to the mountain people that this seasonal transition was hard for some people's health. Even Smiles Like Chipmunk, Green Blossom's sister, was sneezing a lot. Alice recalled that her cough was at its worst when she first came to Bozeman last year, around the same time. She knew she had to lie down and rest more frequently. She felt bad not being a part of everyday activities, but the family understood.

Red had become completely obsessed with making bows and arrows, which was no easy task. His goal of making a big horn sheep bow was going to be slow to complete, mostly because the cold was coming. Red constantly studied the bows on his own, trying to figure out how to piece them all together, but he needed guidance. He had built up the confidence of the clan, and Spotted Eagle decided that he would show Red the necessary skills to craft a horn bow. He warned Red that it would take six or maybe eight months to complete the task. But after the success of his wooden bow, Red was determined. *Apparently he wants to live up to his new name,* Alice thought.

Meanwhile, Alice had been working on her own fall project as the air continued to chill. She put on her moccasins and her cape-like robe for protection from the cold mountain air and she walked over to a wickiup where she and Green Blossom had been making jewelry. She was learning to make bracelets with the help of her sister. Green Blossom had provided animal sinew and cloth strings for Alice, who slowly and carefully tied the strings together in an intricate braid. Green Blossom knew beadwork as well, but that would be the last lesson. Alice started presents for her mother, James, Jed, and even Tom. While she worked, her mind wandered all the way back to New York and to the journey out to Bozeman. She thought of Tom and how his black hair always flopped in front of his face. A smile appeared on her lips.

"I see you still want to go back," Green Blossom said, looking at the accumulation of gifts in progress. Alice shrugged. "I do not want my sister to leave," Green Blossom admitted. Alice leaned over and gave Green Blossom a hug.

"We'll always be sisters, no matter what," Alice reassured her. Then she thought of her mother and her smile faded a little. "Besides, it doesn't seem like I will ever leave. We are so far away from Bozeman, and the winter will be here soon. We've already started to have snow showers."

"Soon, our fingers will be too cold to even make bracelets!" Green Blossom teased, trying to lighten up the situation.

"It's okay, Green Blossom. I am happy here." Alice was surprised at her own words, but didn't feel she had much choice. "I suppose that I am no longer lost. I just have a new home."

"Who is this one for?" Green Blossom asked, changing the subject. Alice had just started a new bracelet. She was being very careful with it and knew it would take some time to complete. Alice was not sure if she should say who it was for. She poked her head outside and looked to where Spotted Eagle and Red were heavily engaged in bow making discussions. With her head poked out of the wickiup, Alice noticed the change in colors with the seasons. She paused and relished the browns, oranges, and yellows around her. She came back in, reassured that Red was occupied.

"It is for Bow Maker," Alice whispered, returning to her work. Green Blossom became quiet and nodded. Alice could hear Standing Rock methodically pounding a hide with a rock to break it in.

"I am working on my bracelet," Green Blossom said, taking out the beginnings of an expertly crafted piece. "I want to make promise," she said, pointing to Alice's wristband.

"I thought you forgot about that!" Alice said, excited.

"I do not forget," Green Blossom declared.

"We'll have to finish everything first," Alice said confidently. "And then we'll take the pledge. I have an idea of someone else I want to include, too."

HOMECOMING

~ *Chapter 30* ~

As James and Tom rode into Main Street, James remembered his arrival in Bozeman only a year earlier. But this time, the town was empty and silent, and everything was closed. This time, there was no Alice, and a fully joyful return was marred by an ever-present gloom. Yet James could not help feeling proud. He had ventured off alone without his family into the wilderness of Yellowstone. He had seen wonders that most grown men only dreamed of—not to mention that he had seen them with some of the greatest and most influential explorers, researchers, and artists in the country.

"What day is it today?" Tom asked.

"Sunday," James answered and nodded knowingly.

"Well, that would explain why everything is closed." They laughed and headed to the one building where they knew their parents would be.

As it was late in the afternoon when they arrived at the small church, the citizens of Bozeman were going off toward their respective homes. The church bells rang, and most folk were clean and dressed in their Sunday finest. It was a perfectly crisp fall day.

"My heavens, look!" announced a shrill voice. "Tommy!" There was no mistaking *that* voice. It was Tom's mother, Henrietta. She greeted them and whisked Tom right into her arms.

"Oh, just look at you. I thought you were never coming back. The Cliftons are so sweet but I thought they were going to kidnap you! And then you ran away with the government men!" She let out a giant guffaw. "Did you get my letters?"

"Yes, mother, they were most informative. I was so glad to know what Mrs. Pease wore to your bridge club last month," Tom quipped sarcastically. She roared with laughter.

"Oh! How I've missed you and that mouth of yours!

You're enormous. You've grown an inch, I think." She pinched his cheeks.

"It's only been a couple months," Tom said, skeptically. "One at Mammoth Hot Springs and one with the expedition."

"The expedition! Thomas, you're on the way to the top! Good heavens, I swear, you have grown. Wait until your father sees you. Your brothers are all here, well, except for Alexander; who knows what he is up to. And I happened to make your favorite tonight: turkey stew with peas!" She let out a big rosy smile. James thought he saw Tom gulp. James remembered how much Tom hated turkey stew with peas.

"See you later, Tom."

"I hope I make it through the night," Tom said to James, holding his hands to his stomach. They smiled at each other through Henrietta's continued ramblings. James felt a sudden sense of loss seeing his friend walk away under the warm wing of his mother. He stood there alone, watching the small assembly of people flow out of the church.

"James!" He heard his mother's voice, finally. Of all the noises he'd heard while he was away—the bubbling brooks, the rustling aspen trees, the crying eagles—

his mother's voice was still the sweetest sound in the world. James rushed forward to where his mother stood in front of the chapel, and they embraced. He took a deep breath and smelled the musty, wooden church mixed with the scent of his mother's soap. James felt an immediate release of all the responsibility he'd been holding the past few weeks. With Mattie's hug, he let go of the pressure to lead the way, to be hopeful, to find something that may be forever lost.

"My boy, my boy," she whispered.

Mattie cried tears of joy and wouldn't let James go. She kept stopping to look at him, her hands grasping his, her head shaking back and forth. Then she was hugging him again, her shawl falling off her shoulders.

"Thank heavens you are home. We are so proud of you," she wept. Mattie took a deep breath and her smile quickly faded. She took James firmly by the shoulders and looked him dead serious in the eye.

"But don't you ever, ever do that again," she said, shaking him a little. "Do you hear me?" James nodded. "If you ever want to do something foolish like that again, you discuss it with me and Jedediah first. Is that clear?"

"Yes, ma'am," James answered sheepishly.

But her harsh words melted away in another embrace, and Mattie's loving face beamed at him once again with warmth and relief.

"Seeing you here now is like a dream come true, like all of our prayers have been answered." She turned and gleefully looked up to Jed.

"Welcome back, son," Jed said, shaking James' hand and grasping his shoulder.

James was relieved that the moment of anger was over and that he was forgiven. *Maybe they really understood why I had to go, after all. And maybe they really hoped that I would find Alice.* Thinking of Alice in that moment allowed his guilt to sink back in. The pressure of finding her would never be relieved, and the welcome home was tainted by the sour absence of Alice.

"How are you feeling?" James asked, concerned, his eyes shyly drawn to his mother's growing belly. Mattie ruffled his sandy brown hair and kissed him on the forehead.

"Fine. Just fine," she replied softly.

When all was said and done, James' journey with the government men had only been about a month, but it felt like a lifetime. They rode home from church in a wagon, catching up the whole way. James told his parents about the mines he visited and the geysers he saw. They didn't believe him when he described Old Faithful and some of the bubbling mud geysers.

"I thought of you," James said to his stepfather, "at the mud pots. I think you would have particularly liked those." Jed glowed.

The front door to their freshly built cabin creaked open. Home for James was exactly how he remembered it, with the additions of furniture and Mattie's decorations.

"We shall revel in our previous works," Jed said. James remembered hammering every nail and laying out every log for their house. He was glad that he had helped build the structure of their domesticity. But the moment of pride was quickly followed by a deep emptiness. The three of them stood there for a moment, all feeling it. Now it was just the three of them. Tom wasn't even there. The absence of Tom's personality and charm was palpable. In the back of the room on a bare shelf was a small box with all of Alice's clippings and toys. James could only imagine how empty it must have been without him there, either.

Chapter 31

ANOTHER PLEDGE

As the winter approached, the clan moved further down the Absaroka Mountains. They camped in the valleys where it was warmer, and where the sheep and other big animals amassed. Food became more and more scarce. Alice's Indian father, Runs with Arrow, constantly complained that the Sheepeaters were hungrier than usual. *Well, they are fighting to survive as outlaws away from the reservations,* Alice thought. *I wonder how long we can do this alone, with only our family.* Their whole network of trade with outside tribes had fallen apart. Their whole system of life seemed to be crumbling before them. Alice had noticed it before, but the winter would be the cruelest time.

As the days got shorter, bad weather threatened their camp. The clan prepared for an approaching November blizzard. They settled near a lake hidden in between the foothills. The family spent many hours putting together sturdy wickiups near some craggy rock at the foot of the tree line in a valley.

Alice, Green Blossom, and Smiles like Chipmunk were given the duty of finding pine boughs and giant wild grass for a bed. They outlined a small area with rocks to designate the sleeping spot. Every night, Runs with Arrow and Spotted Eagle would put a layer of hot coals under the rocks to keep everyone warm. As the snow piled up against the logs and the rocks, it provided additional insulation against the cold.

During the blizzard, everyone huddled together, snuggled against the biting cold. The wind pressed against the wickiup, screaming to come in. Standing Rock started to sing while some of the babies cried. Green Blossom's father carved a flute while he puffed on a pipe, filling the small room with smoke. Green Blossom and Red whispered to each other and laughed, while Alice secretly put the finishing touches on Red's wristband.

Alice had no idea what time it was when she

fell asleep on the warm stones in the center of the wickiup. Her mind was preoccupied with her plans for the following day. *I hope they understand,* she thought as she turned over with anticipation, holding on to Red's completed wristband. That night she dreamt of the secret meeting spot back at Mammoth Hot Springs. Only in her dreams, the gnarled tree was all covered in snow and it floated in the sky.

By morning, the storm had passed over the mountains. Everyone stretched and breathed in the fresh snow smell that had replaced the smoke from the night before. Red and a few of the men went out to make a fire, which was no easy task because everything was wet. Green Blossom gave Alice snowshoes and Alice wandered out with Star Eye by her side. The world was covered in a white, sparkling blanket. The sun slowly rose up as the sky turned from soft orange to a clear baby blue. Alice breathed in the crisp, clean air. The cold pierced her lungs and she let out a little cough. Her cheeks reddened with energy as she marched off and found a small overhang near their encampment. *This is a perfect day and a perfect spot for another pledge,* she thought.

"Come," Alice said to Star Eye, who bounded after her.

Alice went back toward camp to find Green Blossom preparing for breakfast.

Green Blossom smiled with excitement. "You have finished band for Bow Maker?"

"Yes, last night," Alice told her. She had finished the gifts for all of her family first in order to perfect her skills for Red's wristband. "Are you ready to take the pledge?"

"I will finish food. I will get my bracelet and meet you. Come to the cave by the tall trees," Green Blossom said.

"Excellent." Alice said, a smile on her face. She clutched her present close in her pouch and went to look for Red. She found him struggling with the other men to build the fire.

"Red, come with me, I want to show you something," Alice commanded. Bear Heart gave a little look of curiosity. He nodded to Red that he could go. Red looked up at Alice, put on his snowshoes and followed without question.

They got to the cave and Alice suddenly became nervous. Red stood there calmly.

"So, there's this thing that I did with my brother James and with Tom," Alice said, fumbling. She rubbed her hands together. "We took this pledge to protect Yellowstone and its animals and people."

"Green Blossom told me about this," Red confessed.

"Really?" Alice asked, a little disappointed.

"Yes, I hope that's okay."

"That's fine," Alice assessed. "Actually, I'm really glad she told you. That makes me feel even stronger about giving you this gift. Because I think she sees something special in you." Alice was a little embarrassed that she added that last part. Red looked mortified, so she continued quickly.

"I made this for you," Alice said, holding up a braided wristband. Red didn't know how to respond.

"It's not just any kind of wristband," Alice continued. "I made a promise along with Tom and James, who are two of the people I am closest to in the world." She wasn't sure how Red would respond to this because she knew he didn't like Tom and James very much. He seemed to stay interested.

"Well, I was hoping that maybe you would be willing to also take the pledge. Even if you don't, I want to give this to you. You may not see it, but you've changed a lot since I've known you," Alice said.

"Oh," Red said glumly.

"For the better! I see how you treat people, and even more, how you treat the animals. So I wanted to give this to you in honor of what I've seen." Alice reached for Red's hand. She picked it up and tied the wristband around his wrist. Without warning, Red started to speak.

"I promise to respect the animals that I hunt, to use them for their food, to know that they are giving me their lives so I can live mine. I will thank them for their skins and their meat and their bones. I promise to respect them as the Indians do," Red said. Alice leapt forward and gave him a hug.

"I am proud to call you my brother," she whispered. The snow had muffled the sounds of Green Blossom's approach. Alice opened her eyes mid-hug and spotted her in the corner.

"Green Blossom!" Alice said happily. Green Blossom stepped forward.

"This was powerful, Bow Maker," she said, referring to his pledge. Her green eyes were sparkling with tears as she sat down and took out her own bracelet. She handed it to Alice, who wrapped it around her wrist.

"I promise ..." she began, unsure of what to say. "I

promise to teach the ways of my people so they are not lost," Green Blossom stated. "And I promise to speak of your kind hearts for many moons to come."

Alice hugged Green Blossom. Her hair smelled like burnt grass and twigs. They sat there for a minute smiling at each other. They all let out a little laugh. Alice felt the coolness from the rock underneath her and it filled her with energy. The dry, icy wind seemed to speak words of promise, and the power from the cave pulsated in Alice's heart. *These are my comrades, too,* Alice thought. *They understand me.* Somehow, Alice felt James and Tom were there, too.

~ *Chapter 32* ~

BACK IN BOZEMAN

Almost immediately after their return, it was back to school for James. School felt claustrophobic after his adventures in Yellowstone. The chairs and desks were cramped, but there was one good thing about it: Elizabeth. Tom spotted her the first day back, and he kicked James under the table while they were doing writing exercises. Elizabeth swept her brown hair up into a bun during class, but for a brief moment it fell over her shoulders. Tom kicked James again.

"Quit it," James mumbled under his breath, making sure the teacher wouldn't hear. Then Tom scribbled on his chalkboard.

"Go to Crissman's after school?" He drew a little heart, too.

James and Tom had been going to Crissman's to see the photographs from the trip. They were stereo-photographs, which meant you could look into a contraption and see the photo in 3-D. Elizabeth was often there helping him, but James never knew what to say around her.

The last time James was there, Elizabeth told him that she liked to draw sometimes, but that photographs were really the best because they were like the truth. Plain. You couldn't lie or hide anything. She even went so far as to argue that they're the reason the park existed at all. Elizabeth believed that her father and Mr. William Henry Jackson, the official Hayden Expedition photographer who had explored the Tetons over the summer, had to show how spectacular the park was—that it was a land full of wonders—to make people want to protect it.

"I heard from Mr. Blackmore's nephew that one of Thomas Moran's paintings of Yellowstone is actually hanging in the United States Congress," James had said to her the other day in response. "Moran was the official artist of the expedition in 1871, so drawings seem like they're just as important."

Why did I say that? he mulled, sitting at his desk. *Why didn't I just tell her I think she's an amazing artist and that she's right—photographs are better at convincing people of reality?* For a moment, he got lost imagining what he should have said and started staring at her in the classroom.

Elizabeth stopped biting her nails and looked in James' direction. Tom quickly turned the heart-adorned chalkboard over, face down. It made James very nervous. Elizabeth had almost seen it! He kicked Tom back and motioned for him to erase it, which he finally did after drawing a few more incriminating images.

Their first stop after school was Miles' shop. James had to pick up some picture frames for the house and some new ink. Jed was starting to keep a journal and Mattie kept nagging James to write letters to their family in New York, especially his cousin Willard. He still hadn't written to Congressman McCormick.

The town was bustling, and it was no different in Miles' office. When they walked in, James and Tom spotted the McDonald twins, David and Lawrence. The twins were the sons of Richard and Mary

McDonald, two freed slaves who had come from Missouri to make a new life for themselves. After toiling for a number of years as a laborer, their father Richard had saved up enough money to build a two-story house on Tracy Street. The boys were in the shop gathering some goods for the new house. James and Tom hadn't seen them much since their return from the expedition, so they were excited to reconnect. Suddenly they heard Miles shouting from upstairs. David and Lawrence eyed each other with curiosity. They all went to see what the stir was about.

"Fires, fires, fires!" Miles was mumbling to himself when the boys came into the room. There were papers all around. "You would think we'd know how to build a town without things burnin' down, and that people would have brains enough to put out their flames proper," Miles complained. James thought Miles looked like he was a little bit on fire himself.

"I agree," James said, thinking about personal responsibility.

"Well, look who we have again on this fine, delightful, easy-goin' day," Miles said sarcastically. "You know, Clifton, I've had a few people come back and tell me that fires were a problem in your Yellowstone

park." James immediately recalled his conversation with Patterson from several weeks ago. *Maybe they've already spoken,* he wondered.

"It's not my park," James reminded him. "It's everyone's."

"Don't get smart with me, boy," Miles said, pointing his finger. The McDonald boys listened on, intently.

"Do you know why fire isn't classified as a living

thing?" Tom asked.

"Because it's dead," Miles answered bluntly.

"Not really. In order for something to be considered a living thing or being, it has to breathe, usually oxygen," Tom said.

"Don't fires do that?" David McDonald posited.

"Yep. It has to reproduce," Tom continued.

"Fire makes more of itself mighty quick," David's brother Lawrence chimed in.

"Exactly. It has to consume or eat," Tom went on.

"It consumes a lot of wood," James held up his fingers, counting the requirements.

"And it has to leave waste," Tom added.

"Ashes," Lawrence said, contemplatively.

"Right," Tom affirmed.

"So why isn't it classified as a living thing?" James asked, puzzled.

"Actually, I don't know the answer to that one. I just thought of it yesterday. There must be a good way to explain it." They all groaned in frustration.

"Okay, grand. We've moved on to fires. At least you've stopped pressin' me about those darn buffalo," Miles said in his Southern drawl. "More of a Plains problem, anyway."

"No, it's not!" James said.

"Oh great, lookee what I done started up again," Miles said.

"You know about what happened with Bloody Knuckles. And Mr. Blackmore himself went to the Crow Agency and said it was a problem," James retorted.

"I don't care what that fancy-pants Brit has to say. Those British come into our country and think they know everythin' with their pretty words and pretty hats. Dr. Hayden can befriend anyone he darn well wants to in order to get fundin' for his big expeditions. That's fine. I understand politics. But I won't have you comin' in here quotin' some British guest who was tourin' the park. I've too many locals to tell me myself."

"Then I'm sure that you've heard from them as well."

"You're a mighty big pest," Miles said. Tom and the McDonald boys laughed.

"Thank you," James replied. Miles finally put down some of his papers and looked at James.

"What are you goin' to do? The settlers are going to keep comin'. It's white man's nature." The McDonald boys looked at each other with consternation. Miles noticed, but it only fueled his rant. "Okay—It's *human* nature, for cryin' out loud! To find a place and shape it how you want to shape it. If someone's in your way, you'll ignore them or figure out a way to get rid of them, it's as simple as that. It's not wrong, it just is. Do you really think the Indians are all peaceable with each other? Forget it. They were hackin' each others' heads off long before we got here. You remember that. Sure, they're victims now, but they're human too—not some magical peace people."

"Miles, just because it may be human nature doesn't mean it's right, either! And, what about the buffalo? They did nothing and they're useful for everyone. They should be protected regardless of whether they're being killed because of Indians or because their tongues are worth a lot."

"Nope," Miles said. "You're wrong. It's the same as the Indians. Because, see now, farmers and ranchers are just goin' to keep comin' and comin'. And all their sheep and cows are fixed in one place—like us. We come and settle. That's why we're settlers. Now the Indians, well at least most of 'em, are wanderers. Nomads. You ever heard that word 'fore? Nomads. It's a good one. Like the buffalo. They wander in and out of state lines and territories and countries dependin' on the season and on the food. Which is all fine and dandy, BUT you can't have it both ways. You can't be a settler and a nomad."

"But Miles . . . " James started in. He really disagreed with some of Miles' positions, but once Miles got to talking on a topic, it was hard to stop him or change his mind.

"Not to mention the prospectors!" Miles interrupted. "They'll push the Indians out of any place that has gold. You just watch the government try and stop 'em."

Hearing about prospectors reminded James of his conversation with elephant-like George all the way back at the Clark's Fork Mining Camp.

"Say, have you heard anything about Grizzly Ranch?" James asked, recalling that George thought it might be near Bozeman.

"Not a peep. No one's heard of it, like I keep telling you. That George fella you've been talkin' about must have been a few trees short of a forest, if you know what I mean."

James didn't really know what Miles meant.

"He was awful nice and helpful."

"Way to be persistent, boy," Miles complimented.

But there was no more news. Nothing. James had been looking for this place ever since he had returned home and there was still no word.

November was eventful. Susan B. Anthony, the famous suffragist, illegally cast a ballot in New York to protest for a woman's right to vote. And Sojourner Truth tried to vote in Michigan, but was denied a ballot and told to leave because she was a black woman. Men re-elected Republican President Grant in a landslide. Mattie was in a stir about these events for weeks.

Thanksgiving came and went. Mattie's belly was really starting to show from the baby, and the frigid winds set in. James went ice skating and sledding with Tom and the McDonald twins. Before James knew it, December came, and it was his birthday.

James only had one birthday wish: to find out what happened to his sister. Well, and to find out about Grizzly Ranch and its connection to the Long Coat Gang. But James didn't share his wishes with anyone as he blew out his fourteen candles. Nobody talked about Alice—it was like a winter snow had fallen upon them, quieting their discussions. There was nothing to say but to talk about a funeral, and nobody was ready for that yet. *Maybe after a year,* James thought, but he put it out of his mind. He refused to give up hope.

The best birthday present James received was the arrival of a man named Al Jessup. A young man in his twenties, Mr. Jessup boasted a long career of running with tigers in the Amazon and shooting polar bears in Alaska, among many other adventures. But this time, he was going to take on the Yellowstone—in winter! He planned a massive outfit from Bozeman, then a prolonged, extravagant winter trip out in the park. James discovered that Patterson was going on the expedition as a protector from Fort Ellis. James enviously told Patterson to send back letters and keep a protective eye on the park. Miles covered the event excitedly in the *Bozeman Avant Courier:*

THE AVANT COURIER

BOZEMAN, MONTANA TERRITORY   DECEMBER, 1872

TO WONDERLAND—A large excursion and pleasure party, headed by our genial friend Al Jessup, left for the National Park on Tuesday. They propose remaining in Wonderland from one to two months, visiting the geysers, Hot springs and other curiosities of that romantic region. The party, with their retinue of guides, hunters, and servants, presented an imposing appearance as they filed out of town. The road to the Hot springs they intend making up to... crosses the snowy ragged... into some canyons that are very dangerous at this season ... Mr. Jessup is a muchly traveled gentleman having made a tour of the world seeing all the sights of Europe, Asia, and Africa. We prophesy the excursion will be a success for a man who has hunted the Polar Bear in the arctic seas, chased the Tiger in the Indian jungles, and braved every danger of land and deep. Such a man will hardly be turned back by so small an impediment as ten or a dozen feet of snow. The balance of the outfit are all old Western men with years of experience among the Rockies. The boys intended giving the party a parting salute, but when Col. Frank Murray inspected his battery he found that all his pieces were loaded to the muzzle with snowballs. Col. Frank proposes removing those snowballs during the first thaw and give Jessup and his party a booming welcome upon their return.

If only I could get Miles as excited to write about protecting the park, James thought. *I wonder if anyone I know will be accompanying Jessup on the expedition: Baronett or Bill Hamilton, the Bottler brothers, maybe* even *Beaver Dick Leigh, maybe Chen.* James thought happily of his adventures and was envious of the new group plodding out to Wonderland.

But given the hardships that James had faced in the short summer journey, and how difficult the winters were in Bozeman, he couldn't imagine being in the park during winter. Jessup was planning to be there for a few months this winter! *Well, at least he won't have mosquitoes,* James thought, recalling the horrid bug attacks that he'd endured throughout the trip. At one point, he and Tom looked like they had the chicken pox.

"You want to go with them, don't you?" Tom said, standing next to James, observing the parade of Jessup adventurers down Main Street. James didn't have to say anything because Tom already knew the answer to that question. James huffed his breath onto the window of Miles' shop, fogging up a small patch of glass, and wrote the letter 'J' in the frost with his mittens.

~ *Chapter 33* ~

MOVING ON

The winter months passed slowly and early March brought the first thaw. Red was mighty antsy to continue working on his sheep horn bow, but a necessary step was soaking the horns in a nearby hot spring. It was a practical and spiritual experience that could not be skipped.

With his growing influence, Red convinced the family to head back toward Yellowstone Lake where they would find more hot springs. This was risky, as a blizzard could still strike at any moment, and the winter game was leaner and scarcer. But the group had enough supplies and they could feel Red's eagerness.

So the family packed up their snowshoes and set

off for the hot springs, building wickiups along the way. They made big fires and danced at night to keep warm. Alice danced until her lungs hurt, then she sat by the fire and listened to stories. Spotted Eagle walked around in his beautiful wolf robe. Alice laughed to herself about how, just a year ago, she had shuddered at the sight of furs. She still did not like them, but now she acknowledged their usefulness in the cold wilderness, and she appreciated how the Sheepeaters respected the animal that had sacrificed its life for their warmth. Sometimes it got so cold at night that Alice slept not only with Star Eye but with two other work dogs for added warmth.

Red saved the horns of a sheep he had hunted and dangled them around his neck with a buckskin string. These were the horns he would use for his bow. The big horn sheep bow was unique to the Sheepeaters. It was revered for its strong pull and force. The process would take days of soaking and straightening, then shaving and refining with a sharp piece of obsidian, a strong piece of volcanic rock sharper than any known metallic blade. Red would have to use sinew and glue to bind the pieces together and lay them out to dry. Since it was still winter, Red would probably encounter even more problems. But he insisted on the trip. Spotted Eagle told many stories of the old days and how these bows were known by all the Indians for their fine craftsmanship. He was proud to show Red the skills.

Alice thought of how many more months it would take Red to complete the bow and how much longer she would remain with the clan. *Maybe forever,* she was starting to wonder. She looked down at Star Eye, who had grown many inches in the past few months. He still played like a puppy, but she could see him gaining respect amongst the other dogs. She trained him not to jump up on people, not to bite, and how to help carry and hunt. He wasn't carrying her belongings on a sled yet, but she knew it wouldn't be long.

A few miles from Yellowstone Lake, the family found a hot spring and set up camp. It was the same routine as usual. Everyone had his place and carried out particular chores. Sometimes Alice couldn't help because she got dizzy and had to lie down. Occasionally, Smiles Like Chipmunk would get lazy and make something up to lie beside Alice. But otherwise, it was like all the other trips.

One morning, Red excitedly went down to the spring with Spotted Eagle. Alice could only imagine what it would be like. Green Blossom said they tied the horns together and put them in the water to soak and just left them. But Alice dreamed that the horns would grow and stretch out in the hot water ... while Red drew pictures on the stones near the water ... and then maybe the spring would erupt and rain down all the colors of the rainbow, and then ...

"Alice, you are in your thoughts," Green Blossom said. *Daydreaming again,* Alice chastised herself.

"Here comes Bear Heart," Green Blossom announced. He came up and spoke quickly in Shoshone.

"Red and Uncle returned," Green Blossom translated.

"Already?" Alice asked. "But it wasn't that long."

"They saw smoke from a fire in the distance," Green Blossom reported.

The family gathered together to discuss the situation.

"We must go now," Spotted Eagle said.

"It was too risky to come," Bear Heart said in Shoshone. Alice could see that Red felt guilty for exposing the tribe to danger.

"We can come back later in the spring for bows, like usual."

"Did anyone see who it was?" Alice asked curiously. Her excitement was brimming.

Red was quiet for a moment. He stared at Alice and she almost trembled. *Was it Slinger? Farley? Other Indians?* Her mind was racing.

"I did see some folks," Red said tentatively. "And I recognized one of the soldiers from Mammoth Hot Springs."

"Soldiers!!" Alice said with elation, but no one else seemed excited by this news. In fact, they were horrified at the idea of soldiers. They were concerned about how to escape the situation undetected. Six hundred Indians had been rounded up in 1871, and most of them had been put on a reservation in Fort Hall, Idaho Territory. Many were killed. This family didn't want to be on a reservation and they didn't want to get killed trying to escape. They sat and thought. It would take more provisions to go back to their more permanent camp now. It looked like a storm was brewing.

"We will leave tomorrow after the snow," Standing Rock announced. Red looked tentatively at Alice, sensing what was going to come next.

"I think I am going to go," Alice said suddenly, surprising herself and everyone else. There was a moment of silence.

"Go where?" Green Blossom asked.

"Home," Alice replied quietly. "I think that if I don't go home now, I never will." She hadn't cried for months about almost anything. She didn't cry when she coughed. She no longer cried at night when she missed her mother and Jed and James. The longing became an ache that was always there but quieter, lower, deeper, calmer. In this moment, she felt it rising up to the surface like a geyser about to explode. She tried to hold it back.

"I don't want to be lost anymore."

Green Blossom came over and hugged Alice, who started sobbing.

"Okay, we pack up your things," Standing Rock said. "You take Star Eye to protect you." Everyone turned to look at Red to see what his reaction would be. Even Alice stopped crying and looked up to see if Red was ready to go home, too.

"I'll go with you part of the way," Red said. He looked solemn. "To make sure you are safe. But then I will come back. This is my home now." Red paused, then added, "I have nothing to go back to." Alice wanted to be surprised by Red's confession, but she was not. And still, her heart sank into her stomach. Red briefly glanced over at Green Blossom and she looked back at him with a slight smile. Alice understood that Red had not only recreated his life here, he had recreated himself. This was where he belonged, and these were the people he loved. *Of course,* Alice thought. *He wants to work on a bow for at least eight months. He has no plans to leave at all.* It was so obvious to her now that she was alone in her ache to return home. She didn't want to admit it, but she had been alone for a long time.

Early the next morning, before sunrise, Red picked up his walking stick, Alice put on her snowshoes and took a small pack, and the two set off. The clan had created a quiet circle around her, a mixture of smiles and concern etched into their weathered faces. Last to whisper goodbye, Green Blossom reached for her sister. Alice and Green Blossom cried and hugged, not wanting to let go.

"You always have home with us," Green Blossom said.

"You will always have a home with me, too," Alice

replied. They lifted up their wristbands at the same time and laughed through their tears. *I can't believe I am really going,* Alice thought. *I may never see Green Blossom ever again in my life.* She wiped away a tear with the back of her hand.

There would normally be a big ceremony, but the clan couldn't risk the noise or the time, being so close to an unknown group. So the blessings were whispered and the tears were hushed.

Bear Heart's head hung low. Smiles Like Chipmunk, who wasn't very emotionally mature, couldn't stop giggling with anxiety. Alice kissed each baby on the forehead. They cooed and kicked their baby moccasins. Runs with Arrow and Spotted Eagle looked on purposefully.

Alice had so much she wanted to say in that parting moment, but she felt so overwhelmed that the words did not come. She only hoped her gaze carried her thoughts into each person's heart.

The birds were starting to migrate down and Alice had heard a few red-winged blackbirds with the breaking of the day. Standing Rock saw Alice look up to the sky. "Many ravens and birds help people to find lost things," she advised. Alice smiled. Then, in the coming rays of the sun, Alice spotted a mountain blue bird and gasped.

It's a sign, she thought to herself, and felt reassured that she had made the right decision. *My mother saw a mountain blue bird before we came down to Yellowstone.* She thought of Standing Rock's words. *Maybe I am the lost thing the bird has come to find.*

With a final wave, Alice, Red, and Star Eye turned, and they were on their way.

Trudging through the half-melted snow, Alice looked over at her companion. They had been through many things together. She couldn't believe the person he had become, compared to the person that she thought he was when they first met. She remembered how sullen and sad he was back at Mammoth Hot Springs and how James had teased him all the time. She remembered how they were forced to huddle together during the hailstorm and how he had carried her through a fire to save her life. She laughed a little when she thought of how hungry they had been when they dug for roots and then fell asleep clinging to a tree. *I have come a long way since then, too,* Alice thought. *I will miss my friend.*

"Alice," Red said. "I have to tell you something." Alice's heart started to flutter. *What is he going to reveal now?* she wondered.

Red hesitated for a moment. He took out a small wrapped bundle from his bag. "Well, I actually don't have to tell you something, I need you to do something for me. I've kept this with me since Mammoth Hot Springs. I ..." he hesitated again, a great sadness coming over him.

"I need you to deliver it for me, to G-Grizz," he stuttered for a moment uncomfortably. "I need you take it to G-Grizzly Ranch. There is someone important there who deserves to have this. It would just ... it would mean so much to me." *Red would never make a request like this unless it was important,* Alice thought.

"Leave the package outside the cabin; it's better if she doesn't see you. I don't want you to get involved or to scare her." He handed Alice the bundle. She wanted to ask him more about it but decided not to. She put it into her pack.

"I trust you," she said gently.

"Just be careful," he repeated slowly. "I haven't been there in a few years. It got too hard. My pa watched my every move. And he didn't want her to see me. Or maybe he didn't want me to see her, I don't know. I just hope it's still there." Red looked at Alice intently for a moment.

"I promise you, it will be the first thing that I do," she said.

"It's near Bozeman, but hidden. I will tell you exactly how to get there. It's just one cabin, solitary, or at least it was a few years ago. It's a quiet place with a calm stream behind it. Try to go alone. I think it's best if people don't know about it." He reconsidered. "Well, maybe take someone with you just in case, but try to be vague about where you're going. Definitely don't tell them the name of the place. My father told me he was going to build something very secretive there. Here's where to go." As they walked, Red carefully described the way to Grizzly Ranch. Alice repeated it back to him to be sure she would remember.

They stopped talking when they were in view of the mysterious camp amidst the trees and snow. The reality of the situation suddenly dawned on Alice and her legs started to shake. She thought of Green Blossom and tried to be strong.

"Are you sure you want to do this?" Red asked. Alice nodded.

They crept up quietly to examine the situation. The party was quite large. There were a few fires laid out close to each other. *Who would come out here in the winter?* Alice wondered. It looked like some kind of pleasure excursion. She saw a few soldiers, but no sign of anyone she recognized.

"Okay, here's where I leave you," Red said uneasily. "It looks like you'll be safe with these folks. Wait for a few minutes so I can get a head start in case they try to come after me. And remember, don't give them details about the clan." Alice nodded sadly. "You are sure about this?" he repeated. Alice nodded again, but she felt less and less sure with every passing moment.

"One last thing," he whispered shakily. "What I wanted to say, all that way back at Yellowstone Lake,

was thank you for not giving up on me." Red's clear blue eyes revealed a depth that Alice had never seen in him before. They no longer seemed cold, but open and free like the sky. Alice thought of how she had defended him after his tantrum, and kept him calm when they were found by the Sheepeaters. She thought of the pledge that they took together with Green Blossom and the nights they spent together under the stars, huddled together for warmth. In so many ways, they had saved each other.

"Thank you for not giving up on me, too," Alice said. They exchanged one final hug.

She thought she saw him tearing up, but he quickly turned around and traipsed away with his walking stick in the snow. He looked over his shoulder once to make sure everything was okay and lifted his fist into the air, revealing his wristband. *I will always remember him like that,* Alice told herself. He lowered his hand and resumed the journey back to his new family. And then she was alone.

She waited. The sounds of the wilderness were softened by the snowfall. The trees had a heavy layer of fluff coating their bodies. Star Eye looked up at her and whimpered.

"It's okay," she comforted her pup. "Just a few more minutes and we'll go." *I hope I made the right choice,* Alice thought. Red went over a hill and out of sight. *Goodbye, my friend.* She squeezed her arms in a shiver.

Alice was inching in a little closer to camp when one of the soldiers' scrawny dogs sniffed Star Eye and stood up, growling and barking.

"What's that?" one of the men asked, reaching for his gun. Alice instinctively tried to hide, but Star Eye bounded forward.

"Wolf cub!" one of the men shouted. "Let's get him." Alice heard a shot fired and her heart stopped.

"No!" She jumped out. Star Eye came cowering to Alice, unharmed. "Oh, thank goodness," she sighed. But her voice made the men even more agitated.

"Indians!" They threw together their belongings and scrambled for weapons.

"Where?" one of the men asked.

"Right there! There is a little Indian girl," the other man answered.

"No, I'm not an Indian girl," Alice found herself saying. She stepped forward trying to gesture that she was friendly. She imagined herself getting killed over

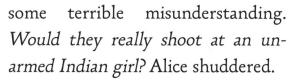

some terrible misunderstanding. *Would they really shoot at an unarmed Indian girl?* Alice shuddered.

"I am here alone!" she shouted.

"Right!" one of the men yelped, "She's a trap!" Soon the whole camp was scurrying for a fight.

"No, I'm not an Indian girl and it's not a trap. I'm lost," she cried.

"Tie her up!" they shouted. A man started to approach her with a rope and flashes of Slinger and Farley raced through her mind. She remembered how they had thrown food at her and tied her up and forced her to sleep on a cold rock.

What if I've made a terrible mistake? she thought with horror.

"No! Please! My name is Alice Clifton and I'm from New York!" The men all paused for a minute and looked at each other baffled.

"Hold up, hold up!" Alice heard a voice from the crowd. A man with a beard and a hat stepped forward. He was a weathered mountain man.

"Did you say you were lost?" the man shouted. Star Eye let out a bark. Alice hushed him but the men's dogs yapped aggressively. All of the horses in camp stomped furiously.

"Yes."

"And what did you say your name was, miss?"

"Alice Clifton, sir." It had been so long since she had used her real name. She almost said Root Digger by accident. Alice looked down at herself and realized how much she *did* look like an Indian. *I should have saved some of my old clothes,* she thought. Her clothes and shoes had long been worn out and used for other purposes, sewn onto other things. She had a feather in her hair and she wore a heavy sheepskin jacket and moccasins. *I can only hope they will believe me,* Alice thought with a burst of fury. *I wish it didn't matter.*

"Well, I'll be darned," the man said. It was Bill Hamilton, the mountain man, guiding Al Jessup's winter junket. "I really thought that Clifton boy just made up his whole lost sister story so he could come on the Hayden Expedition. And look at this ... pheeew," he let out a long whistle. "Put down your guns everyone, she's fine."

"She looks like an Indian to me," one of the men said stubbornly.

"Then she's the most sought-after Indian I know," Hamilton retorted.

"And where did she come from?"

"I told you I was alone," she said adamantly. The last thing she wanted to do was put the clan in danger.

"What's going on here?" It was Patterson! He came running up alongside the young and adventurous Mr. Jessup. Alice recognized Patterson from Mammoth Hot Springs when he went down with their family from Bozeman. She couldn't contain herself. *What if he doesn't recognize me?* she feared.

"Sir!" Alice said. "It's me! It's me!"

"Look who it is," Hamilton pointed. "Says her name is Alice." All of Alice's doubts vanished as Patterson ran up and swept Alice into a giant hug. She shut her eyes tight and didn't let go. *He remembers me! He remembers me!* was all she could think. *They were looking for me! They didn't forget about me!*

"Give her space, boys. Step off," Patterson commanded in a deep voice. The men tossed aside their ropes, embarrassed.

Hamilton came up and patted her on the back as she clutched onto Patterson like he was her lifeboat in a vast, stormy sea.

"Come on, little lady. No need to be afraid. We know all about you. Mr. Jessup will be happy to have you aboard," Hamilton looked over at Jessup, who quickly nodded, despite his confusion.

"We're on the last leg of a long adventure, just heading home now. We've been out here for months, enjoying the great wilds. But I tell you what. We're in need of some new stories," he said. Alice perked her head up and wiped her running nose. "I'm sure you've got some mighty good ones to tell."

She did.

Chapter 34

THE EXPEDITION RETURNS

There was a knock at the door.

"Who could it be at this hour?" Reverend Lawson wondered aloud, making a face at Mattie. Everyone was finishing up a breakfast with jelly and milk. The wooden floorboards creaked under Jed's weight as he looked outside the window and opened the door.

"Tom!" Jed said. "What a pleasure to see you. What can we do for you this morning?"

"Come in, come in," Mattie said, struggling to rise with her large pregnant belly.

"Oh, please don't stand, Mrs. Lawson," Tom said, taking off his hat.

"I just came to tell James that there's a big to-do in

town because Mr. Jessup's party has returned. They seem to be arriving in groups, like we did," Tom said.

"I'm sure they'll be in town for a few more days," Jed added.

"I cannot believe they went out there in the middle of winter," Mattie said as she shook her head.

"Truly testing Providence," Jed agreed. There was a pause.

"Well, go ahead," Mattie said, shooing James with her hand. James stood up and grabbed his satchel. As he exited, he saw Mattie take Jed's hand beneath the breakfast table. After many months of just the three of them, James was used to the quiet in the house. Alice's things still sat on a shelf collecting dust next to Mattie's copy of *Uncle Tom's Cabin*. The St. James Bible that Tom had found at the scene of Alice's disappearance stood stoically still. Her clothes were still in the dresser, waiting.

Town was rowdy—and muddy. Some of the snow had melted and Main Street was a sloppy, dirty mess with the wagons and horses coming through. Some men from Jessup's party went straight to the Chesnut Saloon. Some went back to Fort Ellis. *I can't wait to hear what Patterson has to say about the adventure,*

James thought, looking around eagerly.

James and Tom went to the front of Miles' shop. Miles was standing outside with his notepad, wearing a nice vest. It was a good day for news.

"Hello, runts," Miles said affectionately.

"Any news, Miles?"

"You're lookin' at it," he answered, puffing on his tobacco.

"G'morning," Elizabeth said, stepping out of Miles' shop with her father. They both stood in the doorway.

"James! Tom! Good morning to you," Crissman said in his usual sweet, soft-spoken manner. Elizabeth started biting her nails immediately.

"We heard your voices from inside. Father was here buying some more glass plates for photographing," Elizabeth said.

"We were just on our way home," Crissman said.

"But ..." Elizabeth looked up at her father with her big brown eyes.

"Elizabeth can stay with us," James offered. "We're going to be in the shop for a while helping Miles and listening to stories from the men coming back from the expedition."

"Lucky me," Miles grumbled.

"Okay then, you'll bring her back home, not too long," Crissman said to James and he went on his way with his new items.

"Any news on Grizzly Ranch?" James asked Miles.

"Boy, if you ask me that one more time, your face will be a grizzly ranch. I tell you, it don't exist." *Maybe some of the newcomers will know,* James wondered, not giving up hope.

"Look, there's Chen," Tom said. Sure enough, Chen was sitting on some barrels and talking with a few other Chinese boys.

"Are you befriendin' the Chinese now?" Miles asked, raising his eyebrows. Chinatown in Bozeman was fairly small. It wasn't nearly as big as it was in Virginia City, where a lot of Chinese miners lived. Since it wasn't typical for different groups to mix together in the 1870s, Chinese families in Bozeman tended to keep to themselves.

"He helped guide us on the Hayden Expedition," James said defensively. "And so what if I am?"

"Yeah, so what if he is?" Elizabeth piped up, to everyone's surprise. She furrowed her brow and bit her nails again. Miles grunted.

James called Chen's name and waved. Chen left his friends and came walking over, smiling gap-toothed as usual. He was wearing more traditional Chinese dress than when they had been with the expedition. He worked as a cook and cleaner in the hotels and for some of the restaurants and pubs. Chen's father owned a laundry in town. His mother and the rest of his family were still in China. James saw him now and again in town. They always waved but rarely talked. It was difficult because he couldn't speak Chinese and Chen couldn't really speak English.

"Good day," James said and shook his hand. He introduced Chen to Elizabeth. She smiled and curtsied, lifting the sides of her dress slightly. Miles rolled his eyes.

"Maybe he knows where your Grizzly Ranch is," Miles laughed.

Chen shook his head back and forth.

"See, I told you. No one knows," Miles said. "I've tried everythin'."

Chen continued shaking his head.

"No. No," he said. "Bad place, bad."

"Wait, you do know about Grizzly Ranch?" James asked, suddenly becoming curious.

"What's Grizzly Ranch?" Elizabeth echoed.

"I'm not sure," James said. "I just know that it might have to do with Bloody Knuckles' men, Farley and Slinger." Elizabeth looked at him blankly. She obviously didn't know what he was talking about. "They may have answers about my sister."

"Chen does not know," Miles scoffed. Chen looked at Miles, annoyed.

"I know," Chen said. "Bad. I work, I work," he said motioning dishes. "And boom, boom," Chen said, lifting his hands up like he was shooting a rifle.

"You used to work there?" James was almost shaking. "I've been looking for this place for months!"

Chen nodded. "Secret," he said. "Hideaway. Bad place. Bad."

"Can you show us where it is?" Tom chimed in.

Chen nodded again.

"I don't believe it for one darn second," Miles said. "I'm comin' to see this for myself." Miles grabbed his jacket from the hook inside the door, and his hat from off the rack.

Chen held up his finger to indicate that he would be back in a minute. He walked over to his friends and darted off down the street.

"Where is he goin'?" Miles said. They waited for a little while, watching more of Al Jessup's group come into town. James was scanning the men for Patterson. *He probably went straight to Fort Ellis,* James thought. For a moment he thought he saw him in the distance, but then the soldier veered off in another direction with a few other people.

Chen came running back, out of breath. This time he had a gun with him.

"Come," he said. Tom and James eyed each other nervously.

"M-Maybe you should stay back at the shop, Elizabeth," James said.

"This could be dangerous," Tom agreed.

"No way!" Elizabeth said, folding her arms tighter. "I'm coming." James looked at her admiringly for a moment, until Tom hit him on the back of the head.

"What was that for?" James said, punching Tom in the shoulder.

"Nothing."

"Well, are we goin' to this fantasy ranch or can I get back to my work?" Miles asked, annoyed.

"Let's go," James said firmly, and pointed for Chen to lead the way.

"This better be worth it," Miles grumbled. "I don't like being the tallest person in a group. And let's just be clear here, I ain't no guardian of yours or nothin'. Every man for himself." Elizabeth looked at Miles with a terrified expression, but James knew that Miles would pull through.

~ Chapter 35 ~
GRIZZLY RANCH

Chen immediately led them over the hill behind Miles' shop. Once over the slope, they turned left at a grizzly bear skull. It was hard to find some of the landmarks because of the melting snow, and the house was well hidden, but the ranch wasn't far. *I can't believe it's been here this whole time and nobody knew about it,* James thought.

"Looks like someone else is on their way here, too," Tom said. "Look at these fresh horse tracks."

They crept up to the top of a hill. Down below was the ranch, which consisted of two small cabins.

"Good heavens," Miles muttered under his breath.

They all stood looking out over the scene, and a

sickly silence lingered in the air. It was a truly gruesome place. There were piles of bison skulls as tall as five men. Heads of sheep and antelope were severed from their carcasses, just lying in the snow, their tongues protruding lifelessly. Strung up between two poles were rows of rabbits, wolves, foxes, and badgers, all hanging upside down by their feet. Bloody knives and hatchets were left stuck into tree stumps, pieces of flesh lying about. Flies were everywhere. A wooden placard hung from the top of one of the cabins, with the words, "Long Live Bloody Knuckles" painted with splatters of blood across its face. James felt the hairs on the back of his neck stand up.

"I've seen huntin' for sport, but this is somethin' else," Miles said.

"What a stench," Tom held his nose.

"Bad. Bad," Chen repeated.

"This truly is a grisly ranch," Elizabeth said. She had even stopped biting her nails, her mouth agape. "Look!" She pointed to the left of the two cabins on the other side of the death mounds. "A little Indian girl!"

Sure enough, a little Indian girl in snowshoes carrying a small package was delicately walking across the snow. A uniformed man walked with her. They both looked bewildered by the scene, and the man tried to shield her behind him. The girl cautiously approached one of the cabins with a wolfish, young dog padding by her side. The curtains of the cabin were drawn. There was an old pail outside the front stoop and there were icicles dripping from laundry left hanging on the line, stiffly tossing in the wind. Whiskey crates leaned against the side of the house.

"Strange," Elizabeth murmured. "This is creepy." She went to bite her nails, but was stopped by her mittens.

"Look, there is smoke coming from that chimney," Tom observed.

"Let's get closer," James said.

"I'm stayin' right here," Miles said, settling in near a snow patch on the side of the hill. He took out his note pad and blew on his hands for warmth.

"Fine," James whispered as the rest of them walked down a little ways trying to remain hidden, curiosity driving them forward. The Indian girl and the soldier walked up to the front of the house and placed the package on the steps.

"Is that Patterson with the Indian girl?" James whispered.

"Who's Patterson?" Elizabeth said.

Chen hit James on the arm and pointed into the tree line, where another man was standing guard, his gun erect.

"And Bill Hamilton!" Tom said in an excited whisper.

"What are they doing here? And why are they protecting an Indian girl?" James wondered aloud. It was dead silence as they watched the girl bend down, remove her hands from the package, and very slowly turn around to leave.

"James, doesn't she look an awful lot like ..." Tom started.

"Shhhhh!" Miles quieted him abruptly from behind. But even with the girl's delicate care, a dangerous-sounding dog howled a warning from inside the house.

"Who's there?" James heard the muffled voice of a woman come from inside. Her face appeared at the window for a moment and then vanished behind the curtains. The Indian girl and Patterson pressed themselves up against the side of the cabin to hide, the dog alongside them. Patterson protectively held his arm in front of the girl and kept his gun ready.

The woman came out of the cabin wearing a long, mangy nightgown. Her waist-length hair was red and stringy. She had a rifle by her side.

"Hello?" the woman yelled into the air sharply. "What's this?" She bent down and picked up the package. She unraveled it hungrily, and various items fell out. One toppled into the snow. They seemed to be memorabilia. There was a rolled-up painting, a carving, and a lone bullet.

"Red?" The woman's voice was escalating with feeling as she gathered up all of the items. She fell down to her knees. The little Indian girl was doing her best to hide by the wall. *Why does that girl look so familiar?* James wondered.

The distraught woman sat down and read an etching with a note in it. She let out a loud, frightening sob.

"My son! My son is gone. He's not coming back. My boy, oh my Red!" The sad woman clutched all of the items close to her as if trying to hold on to the memories themselves. She started kissing each of the mementos, crying louder and louder.

"My son—gone! Gone!" The dog inside began to bark louder in response to her cries.

James, Tom, Chen, and Elizabeth were transfixed by the scene. James glanced back at Miles, whose mouth dropped open in amazement. Patterson and the Indian girl remained stuck against the cabin wall. Waking them from their trance, the door of the other cabin suddenly burst open.

"What is she moaning about this time?" a bulky man bellowed, whipping the door open, his hot breath hitting the wintry air like steam.

"It's Steel-Fist Farley!" James said aloud—a little too loud.

"Wha?" Farley said and turned his attention to the group that was hiding at ground level. He furrowed his brow then spotted Patterson and the Indian girl by the house. There was a moment when everything seemed frozen like the icicles that swung from the laundry above.

"Alice, get out of here!" Patterson commanded. Suddenly the silence became a torrent of mayhem.

"Alice?!" James and Tom turned to each other with looks of utter shock.

The red haired woman screamed frantically. "Indians! Indians! Indians!" Her dog wriggled out of the cabin from behind her and ran to attack Alice with snapping teeth. Alice stumbled backward to evade the animal, but tripped on a shovel and fell. Luckily, Star Eye leapt forward, fangs bared, tangled with the mangy dog and bit him on the ear, sending the scraggly creature whimpering in retreat under the cabin.

"Indians! Indians! My Red is gone!" she wailed. The red-haired woman continued to work herself up into a tizzy, screaming. She turned to go back into the house, but while trying to collect the items from the package, she slipped on a patch of ice on the stairs, hit her head on the rail, and fell unconscious.

A long, gangly arm pointed an accusing finger from behind Farley. It belonged to Charley Slinger. "Get the Indian girl!" he yelped excitedly, his eyes bulging out of his face.

"That's not just any Indian girl, fool," Farley said with a growl, raising his gun. "That's the pest we kidnapped."

"I wouldn't do that if I were you," Patterson's voice boomed as he stepped forward and raised his gun.

But before Patterson could shoot, a bullet flew from Bill Hamilton's gun in the forest and hit Farley in the arm.

"Keep that gun down!" Hamilton shouted at Farley. Patterson took the opportunity to spring himself upon the wounded Farley. They wrestled with eager hands, clawing at each other, their bodies intertwined and

squirming.

"Get out of the way, Farley. I can't get a shot!" Slinger said, jumping up and down in goofy excitement.

Hamilton fired again from the forest, but he missed and hit a whiskey crate, spilling its amber contents into the snow. Slinger retreated.

James felt rage burst within him.

"Let's get 'em!" James shouted. In a moment of

sheer mania, he and Tom rushed at Charley Slinger and tackled him to the ground, causing his gun to fall from his flailing arms.

Meanwhile, the two other lackeys from the Long Coat Gang heard the commotion and came running out of the cabin. Immediately upon seeing the uniformed Patterson sparring with Farley in the dirty snow, one exclaimed, "It's a soldier! Oh boy, this is trouble. Let's get out of here." They whistled for their horses and rode off together, but not before Chen took out his gun and fired, hitting one of the men in the bum as he made his escape.

After the dog attack, Alice stood up to flee. Steel-Fist Farley pulled himself away from Patterson and grabbed her ankle from behind. She screamed and clawed at the ground but soon had a cold knife against her throat.

"Look who I have now!" he roared, his neck bulging.

"Leave her," Patterson said desperately.

"Tell me how much she's worth then pay up! We'll get the ransom we earned. If not, she ends up like her friends over there." He nodded to the dead carcasses.

Alice saw the panic in Patterson's eyes, but she remembered Green Blossom's words of strength and tried not to be afraid.

"You'll never get me," she said in a rasp, then jammed her heel into Farley's shin. "Attack!" she shouted to Star Eye in Shoshone. Farley had failed to notice the stealthy threat below him. Star Eye growled furiously and bit his calf. Farley cried in pain. He dropped Alice, who went tumbling into a pile of dead animals. She let out a terrified shriek. The peaceful creek that Red had described was running with blood under the carcasses.

Elizabeth quickly aided Alice and pulled her out of the pile of animals.

"Get up here!" Miles shouted to the girls, and they ran back up to where Miles was stationed behind the hill.

Star Eye's attack gave Patterson just enough time to grab his gun and use it to hit Farley on the head. The blow sent blood streaming down Farley's neck, but as he turned to fall, he punched Patterson in the gut. Patterson bent over in pain from the punch.

"They didn't call him Steel-Fist for nothing," Miles quipped to the girls anxiously from the sidelines. Hamilton fired at Farley again from the trees, hitting him in the leg this time. Farley finally fell to the ground with a thud.

James, Tom, and Chen had managed to pin down

Charley Slinger, who was squirming and squealing like a skinny pig. Chen had found some rough rope inside the house and tied up Slinger's hands.

"Please don't hurt me!" he cried, looking around and seeing all of his companions gone. Patterson caught his breath, marched over, dragged Slinger into the house and tied him to the bed. Slinger abruptly fainted from fear.

Just as quickly as the madness had begun, it ended, and all was silent again. Patterson came out of the house and straightened his uniform. James, Tom, and Chen stood up and brushed off the snow, their faces flush. Everyone assessed the scene. There was nothing to be heard but the sound of the whiskey still streaming out of the crate and the mangy dog licking its wounds under the house.

"It's clear!" Patterson yelled to Bill Hamilton, who lowered his gun and came out from behind the trees. Alice, Elizabeth, and Miles came down from the hill.

"Will she be okay?" Elizabeth bent down near the unconscious woman. Tom took her pulse as Patterson retrieved a blanket for her from the house.

"She should be fine," he said. They all stood there panting. Panting. They looked around at the grisly scene.

Suddenly, Miles let out a huge, enthusiastic, "YEEE HAWWWW!!!" and he started clapping. Everyone turned to look at him with mixed expressions of fear, relief, anger, and exhaustion. "Now that was worth the trip, boys!"

Everyone smiled weakly for a moment and patted each other on the back as if to confirm they were all okay.

Patterson straightened up, keeping in soldier mode.

"I'll take Slinger and Farley back to Fort Ellis with me and keep them under watch. Then we'll put them in prison up at Deer Lodge. I'll be sure the woman is taken care of." Hamilton and Chen offered to stay behind to deal with the outlaws and the unconscious woman. *Our steady team,* James thought, remembering their many days together on the expedition. Then he looked at the Indian girl.

"Alice," James said quietly. "I can't believe it's really you." Overcome with emotions, Alice leapt toward James, embracing him with all her might. They hugged for what seemed like forever, and released months of pent-up tears on each other's shoulders in the middle of the Grizzly Ranch. They cried from the pain of being apart. They cried for how much they had changed. They cried from relief at the capture of Farley and

Slinger. They cried over the ugliness of the battle they just experienced. But mostly, they cried from joy: the pure joy of finding each other at last.

"Me too," Tom said flatly and wrapped his arms around the both of them. The rest of the onlookers, even Miles, got choked up at the sight of the reunion.

"I guess we'll figure out what to do with this disgusting place later," Patterson asserted. They all looked around again at the severed animal parts, including a row of eyeballs on the windowsill of the Long Coat Gang's cabin.

"I-I didn't know what this place was. It was supposed to be a quiet cabin on a stream. I was just doing a favor for a friend," Alice said apologetically. She knew that Red had no idea what had become of his one-time home. It had turned into another killing factory for his father, Bloody Knuckles, and the Long Coat Gang. I am so glad that he didn't come with me, so he'll never know. *My poor brother,* she thought. And then it sunk in. *My brother.* She looked at James again, who had new tears welling up in his eyes.

"But why are you here, James?" Patterson asked.

"This is Grizzly Ranch! I finally found it! Well, Chen found it, actually," James answered, wiping at his eyes with the back of his hand.

Patterson sighed heavily, and put his hands on the kids' shoulders. "Miles, why don't you take the children back home. Miss Alice has waited a long time to see her parents."

Walking back to the house, James was amazed at how much Alice had changed. She looked more grown up and confident. They filled each other in on many details.

"I tried to find you. I went with a government expedition!"

"Patterson told me that on the way back here. Oh James, it was terrible. Farley and Slinger took me and I thought I was going to die. But Red saved me."

"Red saved you? That ... good-for-nothing?"

"He's actually quite sympathetic."

James remembered how much pain Red had experienced at the hands of his father, Bloody Knuckles. He shivered. "Who was that crazy red-haired woman?" he asked.

"I think that was Red's mother."

They didn't stop sharing stories until they finally arrived at the front door of their homestead, where

Alice paused. After all of the fighting, traveling, catching up, and crying, all Alice wanted to do was bury herself in her mother's arms.

"James," she said, "I'm so glad to be home." James let out a big smile.

He opened the door.

Mattie was standing at the stove, peeling potatoes with her back to the door.

"Hello, mother," James said.

"Oh, good timing. James, can you grab me that towel over there?" she asked, not even looking up. "How was Mr. Jessup's arrival parade?" James and Alice didn't know what to say so they just stood there, overwhelmed by the moment.

"James?" Mattie said and finally turned around.

"Hello, mother," Alice said quietly, calmly. They looked at each other. Then Mattie gasped abruptly.

"Alice!" she cried out. She put her hand on the table for support, knocking over the potatoes. But instead of potatoes falling to the ground, it looked like she dropped a bucket of water on the floor between her feet.

"Oh, heavens," she said, grabbing her pregnant belly, "Go fetch the doctor."

Chapter 36

ARRIVALS

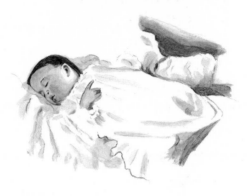

"We would like to welcome into the world Isaiah Lawson," Jed began preaching to the congregation.

"Or, as my daughter calls him, New Beginning," he let out an awkward laugh and everyone joined in. "He is a healthy baby boy. My first child, but not my only child. We are blessed as a family not only to have this new life, but the resurrection of the one that we thought dead. My daughter is a brave girl who survived in the wilderness, and though she was physically lost, her heart never lost sight of the path. We are ..." Jed paused for a minute, getting choked up.

Jed continued, "... so proud and overwhelmed with the grace of God that our little Alice, who doesn't seem so little anymore, kept her heart open to the world and to people different from her. It is that open heart which led her through the darkness, through the fire, and into the arms of other generous human beings."

Alice thought of her Indian family and of Red, of her bittersweet journey home with Al Jessup. She thought of Green Blossom's emerald eyes, and the way her Indian mother would grind seeds to a fine powder. It seemed like so long ago that they were her family. But in her heart, they would always be part of her family. *Why do I have to miss someone wherever I am?* Alice thought.

The congregation listened attentively and all were wowed by the adventures of the Reverend's family. People kept looking over at Alice and whispering, as rumors began to fly about her experiences with the Indians.

Reverend Lawson continued with his sermon.

"And James. James is the kind of person who has the courage to stick to his convictions. His sense of honor and loyalty to family was so strong that he was willing to put himself in harm's way. He fought for every opportunity to find his sister, and that determination brought him into the company of brilliant doctors and scientists. We are forever indebted to them for bringing our boy back home in one piece, and with newfound wisdom."

James reflected on the last few months and all of his experiences. He imagined Dr. Hayden sitting at a desk in Washington, D.C., finishing up his report for the U.S. Geological Survey. He recalled the many nights he sat around with Tom, Chen, and Patterson, telling jokes and stories. Frustrating events like the horses stampeding at night or the pain of hiking up the sides of cliffs now seemed like distant, magical memories from another world. After all of the recent excitement, it felt like a lifetime ago that he had been prancing around Old Faithful, and peering down at his compass in wonder.

"And now, let us sing a hymn together," Reverend Lawson said.

Amazing Grace, how sweet the sound,
That saved a wretch like me.
I once was lost but now am found,
Was blind, but now, I see.

Alice opened her Bible as the chorus of voices echoed around her. She had been so attached to her Bible only a year ago, quoting Scripture almost every day. There were underlines and little stars in it highlighting her favorite passages and psalms about nature. She wasn't sure how she could connect everything she learned from the Sheepeater Indians with all she had known before. She looked down at her clothing, which had quickly reverted to more conventional, non-Indian garb. She kept her Indian wristband on and still had Star Eye, so there were remnants of the old life.

T'was Grace that taught my heart to fear,
And Grace, my fears relieved.
How precious did that Grace appear,
The hour I first believed.

I can't believe this, James thought. *I can't believe she's alive!* James thought of his promise to his father; he had vowed to protect his sister on their journey out West. *But look at her,* he marveled. *She protected herself.*

Through many dangers, toils and snares,
We have already come.
T'was Grace that brought us safe thus far,
And Grace will lead us home.

The pledges that Red and Green Blossom had made rang true in Alice's heart. *Given everything I saw at that Ranch, I needed to come home. There is too much work to be done,* Alice thought. *Grace will lead us home.*

James looked down at his wristband. There were still many unanswered questions, and so much to do. Alice leaned over to him and whispered wistfully, "We have a baby brother!"

They smiled at each other. Even though they knew that they had been physically and emotionally lost throughout many moments of their journey, they had never lost hope.

~ *Epilogue* ~
THE ECOSEEKERS

The next day after school, James called an official meeting. Everyone gathered in the back of Miles' shop.

"I am very glad that we're all here," James began. "After the terrifying scene that we saw so recently at Grizzly Ranch, we cannot sit by any longer. We must come together and fight for what we believe in."

"Hear, hear," Tom agreed.

"This is the first meeting of this group. First, let us do roll call," James said.

"Elizabeth Crissman," he said. "Here," she answered.

"Alice Clifton." "Here."

"Tom Blakely." "Here."

"Chen ..." James tried to think of his last name, but

realized he didn't even know it. "Chen," he said with finality. "Here."

"James Clifton, here," he said for himself. "Even though they weren't at the Grizzly Ranch, I invited the McDonald twins, David and Lawrence." The twins smiled, as Tom, Alice, Chen, and Elizabeth nodded in agreement.

Alice spoke up, "Can we please add two names to that list? Two people who are with us in spirit. They have taken pledges and would have fought at Grizzly Ranch with all their hearts: Green Blossom and Bow Maker, also known as Red." Alice wished more than anything that they could be here for this.

"Yes." Everyone else nodded his or her head in agreement, although Tom was still skeptical of Red's heroic transformation.

"First item of business for our group is a name," James said. "Tom will present an idea that he has already researched for us."

Tom cleared his throat and began: "When James, Chen, and I got back from the expedition, I wrote to Dr. Peale from the U.S. Geological Survey and asked him a few questions. We were all passionate about protecting the park. My favorite tree was destroyed;

pieces of the park were being taken apart bit by bit. We already started to get an idea in our heads that we wanted to do something, not just on our own, but together-like.

"I asked him what some of the latest ideas were about this. He told me about a German man named Ernst Haeckel who, in 1866, first came up with this new term: ecology. It is the science of the relationship between living things and the natural environment. I think this is exactly what we're looking for. So I propose our group be called The EcoSeekers." Tom sat down.

James patted Tom on the back, confident to move on.

"Everyone in favor of the name EcoSeekers for our new group, raise your hand," James said. Everyone's hands shot up. "Excellent, then it's done."

"I just want to say, the real missing piece for me as a new member of this protection group, is to find out who was exchanging the notes with this Bloody Knuckles man," Elizabeth chimed in.

"I agree," Alice said.

"Well, it was signed G," Tom reminded everyone. "I think it's pretty obvious by now, it must be G for Grizzly Ranch. They were probably just notes keeping each other posted on what was happening."

"I don't know," James said. "I think it's something bigger." He thought of how Farley and Slinger had come to their camp during the government expedition. *Who were they meeting with?* he wondered.

"There are still many mysteries to unravel. But the point is, we can't just sit around and despair. Now it's time to do something about it. We can't fight this like children."

"But we are children," Elizabeth said, biting her nails.

"But we have to think like grown-ups if we want things to change. We have to make the grown-ups change their minds. We have to convince them. It's time to take action."

to be continued...

the Real History

Lower Falls of the
Yellowstone River
(circa 1872)

above: Mammoth Hot Springs, lower basins (circa 1872)

right: First known picture of Old Faithful eruption (circa 1872)

below: William Henry Jackson and another man with photographic equipment on a mountain (circa 1872)

Where the Name "The EcoSeekers" Comes From: Ecology

At the end of the story, James, Alice, Tom, and friends create a group called "The EcoSeekers" to protect the environment. As Tom mentioned, the name "eco" is a shortened version of the word "ecology." A few years earlier, in 1866, a German biologist named Ernst Haeckel invented the term "ecology," which refers to the interaction of all living things with each other and their environment. The term literally means "study of the house." Over time, ecology has developed into one of the most important fields of scientific study and provides scientific guidance to help solve environmental problems.

Benefits of Biodiversity: Nature's Hidden Medicines

The wild can hold unknowable cures. Although people in the 1870s did not have the answers, they were asking the right questions. The hot springs cannot cure people of their illnesses, as Alice's family had hoped, but they are a home to special bacteria that can. These bacteria are known as thermophiles (heat-lovers) or extremeophiles (they love extreme conditions). These bacteria revolutionized forensics (scientific tests or techniques used in connection with the detection of a crime) and have many applications in biotechnology, bioremediation (using organisms to clean up pollution), and medicine. Every day, scientists make new discoveries based on these rare life forms.

Where the Title "Lost in Yellowstone" Comes From: Truman Everts

The title "Lost in Yellowstone" was inspired by the story of Truman Everts, as recounted in his memoir, *Lost in the Yellowstone: Thirty-Seven Days of Peril*. Everts was a member of the Washburn-Langford-Doane Expedition to Yellowstone in 1870. He was separated from the group, then his horse ran off with virtually all of Everts' provisions. He survived by eating thistle roots (now known as Everts' thistle), and by

Everts' thistle
(Cirsium scariosum)

using his magnifying opera glass to create fire. After a month alone in the wilderness, Everts was finally found—emaciated, delirious, and frostbitten—by two mountaineers. His misadventure generated an outpouring of publicity about Yellowstone that helped to make the park's creation possible.

Everts was the first choice for superintendent of Yellowstone when the park was created in 1872. He turned it down because the position was unsalaried.

Historical Fiction

Many of the situations that Alice and Red experience, like the fire from the Long Coat Gang, the discovery of edible thistle root, and the shrieking mountain lion, are inspired by events from Everts' story. This is what defines historical fiction: real events and places provide the basis for imagined characters.

Kids & Nature

Once kids and young adults become more comfortable in nature, their fears of the outdoors subside, much like the characters in *The Land of Curiosities.* Alice and Red were certainly scared, but as they continued to experience nature, they learned about it, understood it, and loved it.

According to current-day research and observations of prominent scholars like Richard Louv, it is this initial, underlying fear that has helped to create a modern "nature deficit disorder"—a growing disconnect between people and the wild. This disconnect can be destructive; one of Louv's most influential findings is the potential psychological and behavioral benefits associated with spending unstructured time in the woods and natural places.

But the benefits that Louv outlines are only truly realized when accompanied by an understanding of "eco-values." Red's life-long exposure to the outdoors did not foster a positive connection with nature. It was the power of ideas and values that led to his change and to the creation of The EcoSeekers group.

Kids' Wilderness Literature

Many classic children and young adult literary adventures are survival stories: Hatchet, My Side of the Mountain, Julie of the Wolves, White Fang, Island of the Blue Dolphins, Sign of the Beaver, The Swiss Family Robinson, *and* Robinson Crusoe, *to name a few. These adventures remind us of the incredible strength and ingenuity that humans have when left to fend for ourselves in the great outdoors, just like Alice and Red.*

Children in Early Yellowstone

A man named William I. Marshall, a miner and early Yellowstone tour guide and promoter, claims to have been the first person to take non-native children through the park. He brought his two children and one of a co-traveler for a visit in 1873 and 1875. However, there was evidence of children in the park earlier than that, as described in the diary of 17-year-old Sidford Hamp, dated Tuesday August 27, 1872:

> We [traveled] today 27 miles over mountainous country to the "Mammoth Hot Springs"... We came upon a man holding in his arms the greatest curiosity of all, a baby! ...We got over it however and went on 200 yards and saw two more houses, by this time we were beginning to get used to it, when we came in sight of the springs and 3 houses, and lots of men, women and children.

Sidford Hamp

A 17-year-old British citizen, Sidford Hamp was a part of the Hayden Expedition to Yellowstone in 1872. His uncle was another nonfictional character in our story: William Blackmore, a wealthy British landowner and friend of Hayden. On Monday July 8, 1872, Sidford wrote in his journal:

> I kept guard last night from 12 to 2. It was [very] jolly, the stars shone, and so did the northern lights, and after my guard, I pulled my bed out of doors and slept under the open sky, for the first time in my life, though I expect it won't be the last.

Sidford Hamp's journal was another source used for historical research and an indication that even kids in the 1800s had to adjust to being outdoors.

The Hayden Expeditions of 1871-1872

In June of 1871, Dr. Ferdinand V. Hayden, an influential geologist, set out with a party of thirty-four men, seven wagons, and $40,000 from the government to explore Yellowstone. The result of this expedition was a 500-page report, accompanied by the remarkable photographs of William H. Jackson and artwork of Thomas Moran. This expedition helped prove that Yellowstone had wonders worthy of protection.

Dr. Ferdinand Hayden

After Yellowstone was declared a national park, Hayden returned with another group in 1872. This time the party divided into the Northern Division and the Snake River Division, or Southern Division, as James and Tom experienced. The lists of names from Tom's science journal are all accurate tallies of the names and positions on the expedition. James and Tom traveled with the real Northern Division on the way into the park, and then went with the Southern Division on the way home.

left: Geological Survey en route

left: Dr. Hayden and Walter Pairs, in camp (circa 1871)

below: Members of the Geological Survey (circa 1870)

above: Camp by a small lake between East Fork & Yellowstone Lake (circa 1871)

right: Geological Survey Expedition members at Firehole Basin (circa 1872)

Artists as Nature Marketers

Early photographers were instrumental in creating Yellowstone as a national park and icon. Their works convinced people of the realities of the park. The most famous photographer was William H. Jackson, who went on the Hayden Expedition with the government in 1871 and 1872. A lesser-known photographer on the expedition was Joshua Crissman, who lived in Bozeman and had a daughter named Elizabeth.

Photography and video continue to influence our perception of nature today. Throughout the 20th century, the photographer and environmentalist Ansel Adams, considered a defining figure in the romantic tradition, brought the majesty of the area to millions through his pictures. Today, documentaries like *Planet Earth,* or films like *Winged Migration,* maintain the tradition of allowing people to see breathtaking places they may never actually be able to visit.

Thomas Moran's painting of "The Grand Canyon of the Yellowstone"

Painters were also a critical component in helping the public grasp the natural splendor of Yellowstone. They were able to capture public imagination by portraying places, angles, and vistas that a photographer's lens could not. Artist Thomas Moran accompanied Hayden in 1871, and William Henry Holmes joined Hayden in 1872.

Moran's dedication was equally significant, if not more, as photographer W.H. Jackson's in getting Yellowstone in front of the eyes of congressmen—literally. Moran successfully marketed to get his painting of "The Grand Canyon of the Yellowstone" into the Capitol in Washington. It created a sensation. On June 10, 1872, Congress appropriated $10,000 for Moran's painting, an extraordinary sum at the time. It was ultimately placed in the Senate lobby and became the first landscape in the Capitol Collection.

Stereophotography

Photographers on the 1872 expedition needed a tremendous amount of patience to develop negatives using the wet-plate "collodion" process. Negatives were made on plates of glass that had to be individually coated and sensitized to light before use. The process had to be done very quickly; it was difficult to transport the glass plates and chemicals through the rugged wilderness, and to set up a "dark tent"!

The trend in the late 1800s and early 1900s was stereophophotography, a process resulting in two images superimposed upon each other, giving the illusion of depth, or 3D, when viewed through the then-popular device called a stereoscope. One of the most famous Yellowstone stereophotographs is of men cooking fish in a hot spring at the edge of Yellowstone Lake, just as James did with the Hayden Expedition.

Grand Teton National Park

Unlike the quick and easy creation of Yellowstone in 1872, the birth of present-day Grand Teton National Park was fraught with controversy. Early ranchers and entrepreneurs in Jackson Hole resented expanding governmental control. They perceived the establishment of Grand Teton National Park as an infringement upon their livelihood and land.

It wasn't until 1950 that the present-day boundaries of Grand Teton National Park were established. This effort took three separate government acts, a series of compromises, and local recognition of the economic benefits of tourism. The boundaries included the fusion of the original boundaries of the park established by Congress in 1929, the Jackson Hole National Monument decreed by Franklin Delano Roosevelt in 1943, and parts of Teton National Forest, Jackson Lake, and other federal properties. They also included a 35,000-acre donation by John D. Rockefeller, Jr. in 1949. The Hayden Expedition of 1872 was one of the first government explorations of the area.

Grand Teton National Park

Mining Camps

One cannot describe the 1870s without talking about prospectors. The excitement from the famous California Gold Rush of the late 1840s through 1850s, spread across the country, and many went seeking fortune in the mines. Mining towns sprouted up across the West, mostly filled with men in search of copper, gold, silver, and other metals. These towns usually experienced a few years of boom, followed by decades of bust, as people tested their luck in new locations.

Clarks Fork Mining Camp, visited by the Hayden Expedition in *The Land of Curiosities*, was in a mineral-rich area known as the New World Mining District. It was part of the Crow Indian Reservation, but in 1882 the boundaries of the Reservation were changed and the area turned into Cooke City, in honor of Jay Cooke, Jr., a Northern Pacific railroad contractor. The town fluctuated with the success of the local mines. Today, Cooke City has about 100 citizens.

Repercussions for Today

Abandoned metal mines have resulted in environmental problems, particularly in the West. Run-off from the metal mines seeps into local rivers and streams, and high levels of metal can be traced in fish and other aquatic life. Toxic waters can infiltrate soil and even drinking water, posing threats to human health. There are ways to treat the water, but they are often costly. According to the Environmental Protection Agency (EPA), 40% of the head-waters of western U.S. watersheds have been polluted by mining.

Fire in Wonderland

In *The Land of Curiosities,* The Long Coat Gang started a forest fire, and Patterson viewed careless fires as a tourist problem. But wildfire has played a role in the dynamics of Yellowstone's ecosystems for thousands of years. Fire is both man-made and a natural occurrence; in an average year, about 24 fires are ignited in Yellowstone by lightning strikes.

National Park Service policy currently allows such fires to burn freely as a natural process within the ecosystem, as long as the fire does not threaten people or property. Natural fires are allowed to burn on some public lands like Yellowstone because many plant species are adapted to fire. For example, some of the lodgepole pine trees that make up nearly 80% of Yellowstone's forests actually need intense heat to break open their cones and release the seeds inside. Fires can also stimulate growth of some plants; while the flames consume the parts above the ground, the roots underneath stay healthy and even thrive in the years following a fire.

The summer of 1988 was one of the driest in Yellowstone's recorded history, enabling disparate fires to fuse and sweep across the land. About 1.2 million acres burned throughout the region, and about 36% of the park itself was scorched.

There are differing opinions about so-called "controlled" burns, which are small fires allowed to self-perpetuate until naturally extinguished, under the watch of expert wildlife rangers. One school of thought follows the tradition of the influential conservationist John Muir, believing that humans should interfere as little as possible with nature; the other school of thought believes that humans are part of nature and therefore intervention is desirable. Within these schools of thought there is also considerable disagreement, for example, over the type and degree of intervention.

However, most people agree that the large number of fires caused by careless visitors poses a real problem and threat to the ecosystem. As a result, the National Park Service works very hard to prevent and put out fires that are caused by tourists and human activity.

Hole in the Wall Gang

In Southwest Johnson County, Wyoming, a valley called the Hole in the Wall sits between a red wall of sandstone and the Big Horn Mountains. This isolated area was the perfect hideout for notorious outlaws in the late 1800s. Members of the Hole in the Wall Gang lived in six cabins, grazed their stolen cattle, and provided refuge for other outlaws who passed through the area. Actor-activists Robert Redford and the late Paul Newman played Butch Cassidy and the Sundance Kid in 1969, a movie about a few of those infamous passersby. Newman apparently liked the name so much that he founded the Hole in the Wall Camps in 1988 for children with serious medical conditions.

The Sheepeater Indians (Tukudika)

Sheepeater Indians received their name, Tukudika, because they fed primarily on Rocky Mountain big horn sheep. Grouped among the mountain Shoshone Tribe, along with the Salmon Eaters (Agidika), the Sheepeater tribe was a nomadic group, meaning they never settled in one place.

The Sheepeaters moved in groups of kin, or family. They are often classified as "hunter-gatherers." Women would gather berries and nuts and the men would hunt. The Sheepeaters did not own horses because it was more beneficial to use pack dogs, whose padded feet and agility were more suited to long treks in the rugged mountains. The Sheepeater were isolated and therefore did not have many enemies—they were not a warlike tribe and did not own guns. They were skilled craftsmen, and their bow and arrow was highly revered—Sheepeaters' bows could cut through an entire buffalo and, as Red discovered, the big horn sheep bow took over six months to construct.

*Shoshone Indians
(circa 1871)*

Ideas of Nature and Shoshone Religion

The Shoshone believe in different degrees of puha, or power. The strongest puha was in the mountains. Since the Sheepeater lived among the powerful spirits, they were thought to absorb some of this power. They were regarded as particularly powerful medicine people by other Indians.

The Sheepeater believed in animism. This meant that all objects and places—even rocks—had a spiritual power inside. These spirits in all things controlled the changes in the environment. This made the Sheepeater religion and way of life inherently ecological because all things interacted and were dictated by natural forces.

By the 1870s, the Sheepeater way of life had been greatly damaged. Many had been killed by disease or forced to live on Indian reservations among other tribes.

Sheepeater as Guides

With their intimate knowledge of the mountains, Sheepeater were often used as guides for non-natives going through the park. The most famous Sheepeater guide was Chief Togwotee. In August of 1873, Captain William A. Jones of the Army Corps of Engineers employed about fifteen Shoshones, along with Chief Togwotee, as part of his expedition to explore possible wagon trails from the Union Pacific Railroad to Yellowstone.

Who Owns the Land?

Land ownership was an unknown concept for many, if not all, Native Americans prior to the European arrival in the "New World." As Green Blossom discussed with Alice, the ideas of boundaries around a park or around a state were completely foreign to her. She didn't understand the concept.

In Yellowstone today, officials try to keep human interaction and "natural" interaction separate. But Native Americans see themselves as an integral part of the natural landscape and they often refer to parklands like Yellowstone, which they had traditionally occupied, as holy lands.

In order to create public lands like Yellowstone for humans to observe and explore but not live on, Native Americans were often removed from their homelands. This aspect of American history is difficult. Today, people of various backgrounds are working together to reintegrate Native Americans with culturally significant places within Yellowstone.

Bottler's Ranch,
Paradise Valley,
Montana
(circa 1871)

Concepts of land ownership weren't just changing for Native Americans. Government-owned land for wilderness protection was a contentious and new idea for many Americans at the end of the 19th century. Moreover, people wanted to use the land for private ventures such as cattle, mining, and other projects. But suddenly it was off-limits.

Some people, like McCartney and Horr, who created the first hotel in Yellowstone, tried to work with the government to keep their businesses. Over time, a very profitable business model emerged on public lands; so-called "private concessions" were, and still are, allowed to operate businesses on public lands, usually in exchange for a fee and a commitment to being an environmentally-responsible business. Who owns what property and why remains a hotly debated and difficult topic.

The Tragedy of the Commons

When James tried to stop the tourists from hacking away at the natural formations in Yellowstone, he realized the "tragedy of the commons." This term was coined in 1968 in a journal article written by Garrett Hardin to describe how multiple individuals, working in their own self interest, can ultimately destroy a shared, mutually beneficial natural resource, even when it is not in anyone's long-term interests to do so. As James concluded, what seemed like the best thing for the tourists in the short term would hurt everyone, even the tourists themselves, in the long term.

HISTORY NOTES

The Land of Curiosities: Lost in Yellowstone was thoroughly researched in consultation with historians, librarians, and educators. This included onsite research at the historical archives of Yellowstone National Park and poring over diaries, newspapers, reports, and other primary sources from the 1800s. Additional onsite research and exploration took place at Grand Teton National Park, Wind River Indian Reservation, Fort Hall Indian Reservation, and at various libraries, cultural centers and historical societies in Montana, Wyoming, and New York.

While the story is historical fiction, great efforts were made to ensure the accuracy of the historical settings, places, and non-fictional characters. The following characters in the story were actual people: Dr. Ferdinand V. Hayden, William H. Jackson, Nathaniel Langford, Joshua Crissman, Elizabeth Crissman (daughter), William H. Blackmore, Sidford Hamp, Dr. A.C. Peale, Billy Hamilton, Jack Baronett, Mrs. Pease, A.E. Brown, and the Bottler brothers. The McDonalds were a real family, and the parents were in fact former slaves, although David and Lawrence were made-up due to discrepancies in the historical record regarding the ages of the kids. Background facts and referenced people such as Susan B. Anthony and Sojourner Truth were also real. All other characters were made-up but their experiences are plausible, based on historical evidence.

The lists of names and occupations for the Northern Division (page 49) and the Southern Division (page 156-57) members of the Hayden Expedition are accurate, and were pulled primarily from Hayden's personal report.

The following pages include direct quotes from primary source documents:

page 79 Quote from the Diary of William Blackmore **page 94** Quote from the Diary of William Blackmore **page 111** Quote from the Diary of A.C. Peale **page 144** Quote from the Diary of William Blackmore **page 155** Reference to Hayden speech naming honorary members **page 234** "To Wonderland" is an article from *The Bozeman Avant Courier*, December 1872. Microfiche from The Montana Historical Society.

PHOTO CREDITS

front cover: Nez Perce Encampment on the Yellowstone River: photo by William H. Jackson, 1871: Courtesy of the National Park Service. **back cover** Dr. Ferdinand V. Hayden: photo by William H Jackson, 1871: Courtesy of the National Park Service. Shoshone Indians: photo by William H Jackson, 1871: Courtesy of the National Park Service. Geological survey en route: photo by William H Jackson, circa 1872: Courtesy of the National Park Service. Members of Survey: photo by William H Jackson, circa 1870: Courtesy of the U.S. Geological Survey. Lower Falls of the Yellowstone: photo by William H. Jackson, circa 1872: Courtesy of the Library of Congress. Mammoth Hot Springs, lower basins: photo by William H. Jackson, circa 1872: Courtesy of the Library of Congress. **page 288** Lower Falls of the Yellowstone: photo by William H. Jackson, circa 1872: Courtesy of the Library of Congress. **page 289** Mammoth Hot Springs, lower basins: photo by William H. Jackson, circa 1872: Courtesy of the Library of Congress. Old Faithful eruption: photo by William H. Jackson, circa 1872: Courtesy of the National Park Service. William Henry Jackson and another man with photographic equipment: photo by William H Jackson, circa 1872: Courtesy of the Library of Congress. **page 291** Everts' thistle: photo by J. Schmidt, 1977: Courtesy of the National Park Service. **page 294** Dr. Ferdinand V. Hayden: photo by William H Jackson, 1871: Courtesy of the National Park Service. Geological survey en route: photo by William H Jackson, circa 1872: Courtesy of the National Park Service. **page 295** FV Hayden & Walter Pairs: photo by William H Jackson, 1871: Courtesy of the National Park Service. Members of Survey: photo by William H Jackson, circa 1870: Courtesy of the U.S. Geological Survey. Camp by small lake: photo by William H Jackson, 1871: Courtesy of the National Park Service. Geological Survey Expedition: photo by William H Jackson, 1872: Courtesy of the National Park Service. **page 296** The Grand Canyon of the Yellowstone: painting by Thomas Moran, 1872: Courtesy of the the Department of the Interior. **page 298** Grand Teton National Park. Courtesy of the National Park Service. **page 300** Yellowstone fire of 1988, near Old Faithful. Courtesy of the National Park Service. **page 302** Shoshone Indians: photo by William H Jackson, 1871: Courtesy of the National Park Service. **page 304** Bottler's Ranch, Paradise Valley, Montana: photo by William Henry Jackson, 1871: Courtesy of the National Park Service

Please visit our website, www.theecoseekers.com, for additional resources.

ACKNOWLEDGEMENTS

We would like to thank:
All of our endorsers, Lee Whittlesey and everyone at the Yellowstone Heritage
and Resource Center, the Yellowstone Association, the Grand Teton Natural
History Association with a heartfelt shout out to everyone at the Moose Visitor Center,
The Montana Historical Society, Dubois Museum, Wind River Historical Center,
The Museum of the Big Horn Sheep, Shoshone Cultural Center,
New York Public Library, Erminio D'Onofrio—Head of Information Services at the
New York Public Library, Brooklyn Public Library, The United States Geological Survey,
Peter Nabokov, Lawrence L. Loendorf and Nancy Medaris Stone
for their book *Mountain Spirit: The Sheep Eater Indians of Yellowstone,*
Leslie Hoffman and the Jackson Religious School at Sutton Place Synagogue,
Steven B. Jackson—Adjunct Professor of Photography, Department of Media and
Theatre Arts at Montana State University, Phyllis Smith, Mike Mease and
The Buffalo Field Campaign (a special thank you for the overnight accommodations
and hospitality), Jim Posewitz and Orion—The Hunter's Institute, Becky Bercier,
Mark, and the Wind River Business Development Program, Lee Silliman, Jim Stone at
the Inter-tribal Bison Cooperative, Matthew McLean at Old Faithful Inn, Jim Horan
at Canyon Lands, Peter Kandell at Four Winds, Rebecca Humrich, Mike Yost, Kyle and
everyone in distribution, and Michele Mitchell who should be running the Office Depot.

Most importantly, thank you to everyone who worked so hard to bring this book to print:
Paula Winicur, Sandra Winicur, Christy Kingham, David Erickson, Tom Newsom,
David Lowe, Sylvia Neil and Dan Fischel, Nicole Tugeau, Tom Mendola, Adam Fanucci,
Christopher Madden, Rachel Billow, Naomi Newman, David Chapman, and
Jennifer Hissom! And, thank you to Daniel Frohling, Seth Rose,
and Angela Ocasio—all of Loeb & Loeb.

A special thank you to our family:
to Laura for making Dave so happy; to our Dad (Mark) and Mom (Sylvia),
for raising us with a deep appreciation for nature through trips to national
and state parks (and for facilitating an awesome brother-sister bond,
all those noogies aside), and to everyone in our family—Dan Fischel, Joey,
Matt, Sarah, Gramps, Jojo, and Doug and Wendy Kreeger—for continuing
to foster and share our deep appreciation for the great outdoors.
We cannot express enough gratitude for your love and support.

This book is dedicated to Elijah Hayes Neil, Miles Benjamin Neil,
Henry Judah Neil, and to all the generations that are to come.
May you learn from the past to help create a better future.

DEANNA NEIL is an award-winning author, playwright, singer, educator, and journalist. She has been featured in *USA Today, ABC News,* and *Time Magazine for Kids* named her a 2008 "Hero for the Planet." Deanna currently lives in Los Angeles, and frequently visits Yellowstone National Park and Grand Teton National Park.

Conceived by **DAVID NEIL**, The EcoSeekers was founded in 2006 by the brother-sister duo of David and Deanna to entertain and inspire the next generation of environmentalists. The company was awarded "best first book" (silver) by the Independent Publishers Association, and has been featured on *Good Morning America Now.*

David is a longtime champion of children's literacy, and is a recipient of the Celebrate Literacy Award from the International Reading Association. David is a real estate executive in New York City and the proud father of three boys. He considers The EcoSeekers his fourth child.

David and Deanna in Alaska, August 2001